Jim Stewart's JAPAN:
Sake Breweries of Tokyo, Kyoto, and Kobe

Jim Stewart's JAPAN:
Sake Breweries of Tokyo, Kyoto, and Kobe

JIM STEWART

Advanced Sake Professional

ISBN 13: 978-1-60332-117-4

Cover design by Kursti Martinsen
Book design by Sue Balcer

Table of Contents

Special Thanks

Thank you Farrah for your trust and forbearance while I was away doing the Very Serious Work (in Japan drinking sake).

Thank you Paul and Seiko for taking care of me in Japan.

A book such as this can only be written by a team and my contributors – the famed sake blogger down under Slava Beliakova, and man on the ground Ian Anderson deserve credit for their inspired work. Thank you both.

Visiting Sake Breweries in Japan

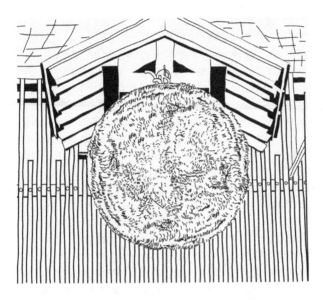

This book is about travel in Japan and one of my favorite things to do in there: drink sake and visit the places where it's made. Like visiting a winery when you're in California, Italy, France, or Australia – if you're like me, your visit to a sake brewery in Japan will be the highlight of your trip, and the experience you'll tell your friends about when you return home.

Some travelers, despite having "been everywhere", manage to skip Japan. This is a big mistake. Japan is the land of sumo, sake, sushi, samurai, kabuki, and geisha – and is also a land overflowing with graciousness, decency, and an attention to detail in all things that will delight the jaded and cynical world traveler. Remarkably, it's also a budget travel destination. When approached with the right mindset, you can travel well in Japan for far less than you might spend in Europe. Japan is also filled with things familiar to the West: baseball, light beer (if that's your thing), fried chicken, and ... the English language. Don't be intimidated: when you visit Japan, you'll be able to travel well without learning how to read Japanese characters.

Many of the comforts and necessities of life will be familiar. But I promise you will also be surprised by a few things.

Take a moment to contemplate a common scene: An airport shuttle bus pulls alongside the curb at a busy airport, and the ticket-taker doesn't smack her gum or yell at you for standing in the wrong place. After punching your ticket and helping you with your bags (which you'll get a receipt for), she bows deeply to the bus as it comes to rest. Is she honoring the machinery? After you board the bus, she then bows for *you ... and everyone else on the bus* before you depart. This isn't a joke. Things are different in Japan. So please take a quiet moment and make a personal commitment that on this trip, you'll open your mind and try to acknowledge the decency so often on display in Japan and promise yourself that you'll reciprocate.

Japanese people are honestly dedicated to the idea that cooperation and harmony in all things is something to be honored. And now you've just read a word that you don't see much in the West. Honor. It means something in Japan.

Just smaller than the state of California in size, Japan's 128 million people have found a way to live in harmony – and Tokyoites with more than 13 million fellow residents live in the largest metropolitan city *in the world*. And they live well. Be prepared to be delighted by the small things that are done well in Japan. From the vending machines that serve hot and cold beverages – and are all in perfect working order – to the food in the corner convenience stores. It's fresh and cleverly packaged. The trains run on time.

When you visit Japan, try to visit as many of the sake breweries in this guidebook as possible. Your efforts will be rewarded. Tell the owners you're visiting and that your friend Jim sent you. You'll be welcomed into the international family of sake drinkers – with a warm smile and more than a few glasses of delicious sake. You might also, as I have, make many new lifelong friends along the way. The world of sake, and Japan in general is still that kind of place.

A Quick Note on Brewery Selection

This is a travel guidebook first. My goal is to make it easier for you to visit a sake brewery or two when you visit Japan. But are these the only breweries in Japan? Are they the best? To say "far from it" is an understatement. I've selected these breweries personally, and each for different reasons. Perhaps they have a very nice museum, or they may be global brands with which you should be familiar as you start drinking more sake. It's fun to return home and see familiar names on the menu.

But in the end, the breweries in this book have been carefully chosen so that when you're visiting Tokyo, Kyoto, or Osaka, you should find that visiting a brewery or two fits quite easily into your travel itinerary.

You may also find that the number of breweries covered in this book is quite modest. My aim here, of course, is to help narrow your choices and provide detailed information about how to get where you're going. I've visited each of these plac-

es personally, and have painstakingly made maps and written directions so that none of your precious travel time is wasted. You may plan and travel with confidence, knowing your brewery visit will deliver maximum delight for the time you allocate to a visit.

Finally, by some estimates, Japan supports 1200 working sake breweries. Inclusion in this book should in no way diminish the work being done by those left out – there are some very historical, secretive, wonderful and culturally rich places that are simply not included here. I encourage you to seek these out. If you visit a brewery and have a splendid experience, please drop me a line and let me know what you found! I'll try to visit myself and perhaps include your favorite place in the next edition of this book.

Reservations, Please

I often talk about how different Japan is from the West in terms of honor and decency. And these days, in terms of personal saftey, Japan is second to none. You are very unlikely to be the victim of any sort of crime while in Japan. There are many theories behind how and why Japan is so safe and how Japan has developed such a cohesive society -- Japan is not without its own problems, of course, but one of the things that keeps floating to the surface is, frankly, manners. Saying please, thank you, that was a nice meal -- all of these things are a part of Japanese society and I hope you will consider yourself an ambassador of sorts from your own country when you visit Japan, remembering to show them your best manners when visiting.

More than most place you may visit, good behavior in Japan means announcing your arrival in advance of your visit. Many of the breweries in this book are big companies that are set up with museums and tasting rooms and can accommodate visitors unannounced, but I have found that a tiny bit of effort goes a long way in Japan. Reservations are customary, and a courtesy I hope you can extend, so that we don't wear out our welcome visiting these generous brewers who are so happy to serve as our hosts in Japan.

If you can make a reservation on the brewer's website, or drop them a simple email letting them know about your plans to visit, you may be thrilled by their response-- "we'll pick you up at the train station" is not infrequent, or "we'll have a special tour ready for you," or "yes, we are so happy for you to come taste our sake."

Also important to note is that sake brewing is a tough business in Japan, and you may find that they would rather have you come on one day rather than another -- sake tourism is really in its infancy, so for all breweries in this book, your experience will be that much more meaningful and wonderful (and perhaps more convenient for our hosts) if you can reach out to the brewers before your arrival and make some plans. Writing ahead for a reservation will also help avoid disappointment - it is one simple thing we can do to be the best ambassadors possible for our home countries and to really increase the chances of us having a wonderful sake brewery tour while we're in Japan. Write the brewery a quick note expressing your interest in visiting – and prepare to be amazed at what happens next.

A General Note on Sake and Japanese Culture

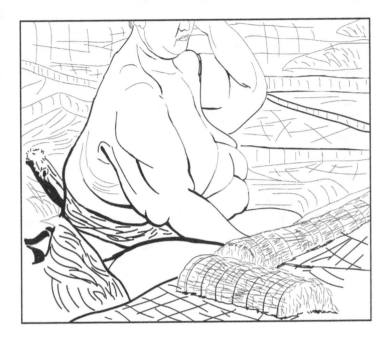

As you start planning your trip to Japan, you'll notice layers of meaning and depth associated with just about everything. History and tradition are rich in Japan and they're everywhere you look. Names and their meanings are delightfully ambiguous. As you try to find answers, many are readily available – others remain elusive.

It is one of those things that will keep you returning to Japan year after year – curiosity and study are richly rewarded.

Sake is no exception. It's a big topic. Sake has played a central role in Japanese life and cuisine for the past 2000 years. Therefore, the study of sake means the study of Japanese history, culture, society, cuisine, as well as the social environment of Japan today.

Therefore, I cannot claim to do the subject of sake justice in the few pages provided here. There are many authors and books on the topic, and I would encourage you to pursue titles such as:

The Sake Handbook by John Gauntner

Sake's Hidden Stories by John Gauntner

Sake Confidential: A Beyond-the-Basics Guide to Understanding, Tasting, Selection, and Enjoyment also by John Gauntner

My focus is to provide you with the tools needed to facilitate visiting sake breweries while on a trip to Japan, and also to help you order and enjoy sake on your vacation ... and ... if I'm successful ... perhaps you'll start drinking more sake when you return home!

A Brief History of Sake: Monks, Emperors and Samurai.

Having found a 12,000 year-old earthenware jar containing an abundance of wild grape seeds somewhere near modern Yamanishi (another of my favorite parts of Japan) in 1958, Japanese historians believe that the oldest alcoholic beverage produced in Japan is actually ordinary grape wine. If this scholarship is to be believed, this could be the earliest record of wine making anywhere in the world.

A prolific monk describes an early form of sake made by people spitting chewed up rice into a vessel, and letting the rice and saliva mash ferment. Interesting though this may be, sake making didn't begin in earnst until 1000 to 300 BC, after the arrival of greatly improved rice cultivation techniques.

Thankfully, the sake we know now wasn't made until the late 7th century. It's during this time that the koji, the mold that breaks down rice starches into sugars in sake production, was introduced. The origin of koji is unclear- some believe it was imported from China, while others think the mold was discovered in Japan.

Fast forward 100 years and we find ourselves in Nara, the capital of Japan from 710 A.D. Nara became the first center of sake brewing. In fact, the business of sake became so serious here that the government of the time set up a brewing department to regulate and systemize the craft.

Nara wasn't just the center for sake brewing and the Emperor's seat of government. It was also the center of the increasingly powerful Buddhist clergy. Like today, clergy back then weren't ones to pass on a lucrative business opportunity, and many temples took up sake brewing.

Uncomfortable with the growing number of powerful temples in Nara, the emperor Kammu moved the capital to nearby Kyoto, and the sake brewing industry followed. Japan entered its Golden age. The aristocracy dedicated their leisurely days to artistic and aesthetic pursuits, and sake accompanied their seasonal and religious ceremonies. Records show numerous Kyoto artisans were contracted by the imperial court to make sake. By the 13th century, there were over 300 breweries.

Kyoto Buddhist monasteries, just like the monasteries of Nara, also continued to brew sake. The monks, for whom focus and concentration were their life's work, approached sake brewing with the same degree of attention. They continuously perfected the art and craft of sake brewing until by the eleventh century, Kyoto temples created the brewing system very similar to the modern-day one. Sake as we know it today, therefore, is about a thousand years old.

Kyoto, hundreds of years ahead of other places, remains one of the most important sake-producing regions in Japan.

While the courtiers composed haiku and admired cherry blossoms, the provincial warriors – the early samurai – grew more powerful. In 1185, the first shogun received his title and Japan entered the age of the warrior state. Eventually, the military government began taxing sake and encouraged its mass production, as it was an important source of revenue. At the same time, the samurai viewed temples as power rivals, and destroyed many of them. By the sixteenth century, sake brewing shifted from shrines and temples to commercial breweries, and spread outside Kyoto.

Kobe, a seaport near Osaka, became an important brewing region, as sake from there could be quickly transported by ship to Tokyo (then called Edo). Edo was the seat of government power at the time and it was a thirsty city! One area of Kobe in particular, Nada, came into prominence. Proximity to the shipping route to Tokyo was one advantage, but the biggest reason for the success in sake brewing was the discovery of Miyamizu, shrine water, in Nada. Sake brewed with Miyamizu was (and is) of remarkably high quality. Since the Edo period, Nada has continuously remained the top brewing region of Japan.

Despite sake's long and fascinating history, it is during the 20th century that sake brewing underwent the most dramatic transformation. Technological advances such as rice milling, stainless steel fermentation tanks replacing cedar, and the isolation and discovery of modern fragrant yeasts spurred the development of today's elegant, refined, delicious sake.

Sake Basics – Know at least this much

Sake, not "saki" or "sackey" – is pronounced as "saw kay" – and in Japan is known as Nihonshu. Nihon = "Japan," and shu = "drink" ... therefore literally "Japan drink." When you visit Japan, the word takes on a much more ambiguous meaning akin to "alcoholic drink"; if you were to ask someone if they loved sake, they'd be likely to say "of course! I love it!" Pressing a new friend on the matter of their taste for "nihonshu" would be more accurate, and you may make a friend for life if you do find a sake enthusiast. However, for the purposes of this book we'll consider the words sake and nihonshu to be one and the same.

Sake is made primarily from rice and water. It is made much more like beer than wine - it is not the product of a simple fermentation like wine and so calling sake "rice wine" is technically incorrect.

Sake is brewed using a microorganism called koji and

yeast. When finished, sake typically has an alcohol content of between 13% and 16%.

There are many different varieties of sake and while it can be enjoyed warm or cold, many premium sake – particularly the kind that have been rapidly growing in popularity in the West – are best drunk slightly chilled.

For the consumer, one of the most exciting things about sake is that there are some objective criteria by which you may empirically judge and purchase it. That is to say, most of the time there is a direct linear link between quality and price. There are several factors to consider when purchasing sake, but one word stands alone in helping you understand the word of premium sake.

That word is GINJO.

A ginjo is sake made from rice that has been milled down to at least 60% of its original grain size. There are many things that make ginjo interesting and wonderful, but if you're new to the world of sake, you might want to ask for "ginjo-shu" or think about ginjo as your gateway into the world of premium sakes.

Another important word in sake is "junmai", which translates to "pure rice" – again, an empirical designation and legal definition for sake which has been produced with rice and rice alone.

While makers of ginjo may add a smidgen of brewers alcohol, added just before pressing the fermented mash to bring out aromatic esters that are not water soluble, but it is important to note that brewers alcohol is never used as fortification of the sake. If you're drinking a junmai, you're drinking a sake that has been produced in this pure fashion without the benefit of this flavor extraction.

Some rules of thumb:

Ginjo – Easy drinking, often more refined, delicate floral notes.

Junmai – At time more fragrant, stands up to heartier fare.

Kimoto & Yamahai – gamier, using wild lactic acid producing bacterium for portions of their fermentation.

How to drink sake - Vessels

Why is sake drunk out of those tiny little cups?

Half of the fun of drinking sake is the cultural experience. Traditionally, sake is served in small earthenware, porcelain, or lacquerware cups called "choko", and depending upon their shape and size may require frequent refilling. One of the most interesting (and most delightful) traditions for drinking sake is that one does not fill his or her own glass – you must attend to your fellow companion's needs and they must attend to yours. Your friends will pour for you, and you will pour for your friends. Hopefully you get the picture – Japan loves consideration and harmony. Why not double down on the sheer joy and warmth of a shared experience like drinking sake with a new friend? That's how they do it in Japan.

Keeping the cup sizes small facilitates more frequent sharing and the pleasure that accompanies giving and receiving.

Ochoko (adding the honorific "o" makes "o-choko") are made all over Japan and you'll notice different names associated with the vessels of various shapes and sizes. Some regions have distinct pottery styles, highly prized among art collectors. For example, a single Bizen in Okayama or Shigaraki in Shiga can command thousands of dollars.

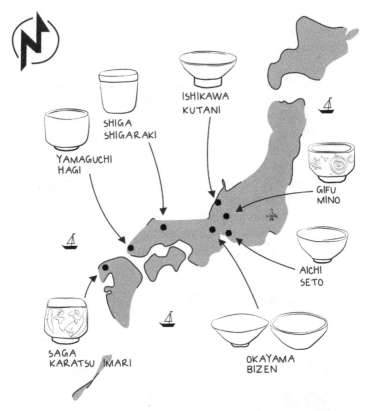

You'll notice some sake vessels that closely resemble a saucer – these are more properly called "sakazuki" and are used in celebrations and rituals, including yakuza initiations. You'll find sakazuki made of precious metals and indescribably gorgeous lacquerware ... with corresponding prices for those interested in acquiring a souvenir.

Drinking sake out of ochoko is an aesthetically pleasing experience.

You'll find the different drinking vessels available in Japan wonderfully tactile, warm, and interesting-looking, so they definitely appeal to several senses of the drinker.

I recall sharing a lunch with a producer of fine sakazuki at her home in Kobe, enjoying refined aristocratic daiginjos – and a spirited sake drinking session in a crowded, smoky food market in Kochi over far humbler brew. And I can tell you – how and where you drink sake are just as important as what you're drinking. My advice: go to Japan and try as many different kinds as you can.

Unglazed cups will suit sturdier junmai style, while lacquered and polished cups will be more appropriate for delicate and fragrant ginjos.

Vessels are roughly divided into 2 sizes. Choco (ochoko) is a small cup, often used for drinking warm sake. Guinomi is a medium-sized cup sometimes used for chilled sake. Choco will often (or, in case of warm sake, always) be accompanied by a small matching bottle, tokkuri, 150-300 ml in size. You will have a lot of fun pouring sake out of tokkuri into your dainty cups – a hard-to-beat and authentic Japanese experience!

Invest in a good quality set (or two) while you're in Japan and recreate the izakaya atmosphere when you're back home.

Glass

For slightly chilled sake, glass vessels are great. Sake glasses in Japan are traditionally rather small, perhaps shaped like elongated shot glasses or a Japanese drum. Modern bars and restaurants often serve sake in wine glasses. The shape of a wine glass is ideal for aromatic ginjo styles, letting the fragrance spread over the wider surface, then funneling it towards the drinker.

Burgundy wine glasses will enhance the fruity aromas of very fragrant sakes, and flute-shaped glasses will concentrate the refreshing aromas of light and dry sakes.

Glass doesn't just help with experiencing fragrance. The thin lip of the glass changes your flavor perception ever so slightly, making the palate more receptive.

Other sake ware

Many people associate sake drinking with small white porcelain cups with blue rings drawn on the bottom inside. This is **janomeno kikijoko**, the traditional sake tasting cup. The blue rings are there to help discern the clarity and color of sake during the tasting. Despite their popularity in the West, you are very unlikely to come across kikijoko in a Japanese pub. Truthfully, the fat porcelain lip and dull design will not add anything to your drinking experience.

On the other side of the spectrum, there is **kiriko,** less common (and quite expensive) colored crystal sake ware with cut designs on the surface. Two design styles, Edo Kiriko (Tokyo kiriko) and Satsuma Kiriko (kiriko from Kagoshima prefecture) are particularly popular.

Here is one of my favorites: lacquerware.

A traditional Japanese art, lacquerware is both painstakingly produced and undeniably gorgeous. I was a skeptic at first but laquerware is incredibly light. You're holding what you're expecting to be a substantial vessel but the laquerware is light as a feather.

Tasting ginjo by Osaka bay with laquerware sakazuki is simply one of those peak life experiences. Pick up a set of your own traditional, gorgeous lacquerware sakazuki and join the cognoscenti.

Hot or Cold?

Many people come to sake by way of trying some piping hot brew in their neighborhood Japanese restaurant. If that experience didn't scare you away, kudos to your curiosity. As more and more people become aware of the premium spectrum of sake, hot sake is becoming a symbol of cultural ignorance.

But not so fast. Heating sake is a legitimate and very traditional way to drink sake. You will encounter hot or gently warmed sake at the wonderful winter matsuri (Chichibu Yo-matsuri comes to mind). You have to remember, though, that

ginjo (remember, one type of premium sake) wasn't really brewed on a commercial scale until the 1970s. In the olden days, when sake was a rougher and sturdier stuff, heating it did mellow its flavor. The perception of sweetness increases until sake reaches about 37 degrees, then drops off. And there is nothing like coming in from the cold and warming yourself with a nicely heated ochoko or two of sake.

Warming premium sake can also be a conscious, valid choice. Full bodied sake, particularly junmai and yamahai styles, often benefit from a gentle warming up. Their aromas "open up" and become more pronounced, and the sake itself becomes sweeter and mellower.

Warming is not recommended for the fruity, aromatic ginjos or zingy namazake, as the delicate aromas and freshness will be lost.

The Japanese have a name for each temperature of warmed sake. Try asking a brewer or barkeep for sake at one of these temperatures. They'll be surprised (and delighted)!

Hinata-kan	Warmed in the sunshine	30° C
Hitohada-kan	Heated to body temperature	35° C
Nuru-kan	Heated to tepid temperature	40° C
Jo-kan	Heated to fairly warm	45° C
Atsu-kan	Heated hot	50° C

Learning the Japanese Kana

I like to cultivate the idea that when you visit Japan, especially for the first time, you shouldn't worry too much about speaking (or not speaking) or understanding written Japanese. Also, you really shouldn't have any anxiety about understanding the Japanese alphabets, collectively called the kana. You should get along quite nicely and enjoy with confidence a couple of weeks in Japan without any knowledge of the Japanese language whatsoever. I have sent many of my friends and family members to Japan, and despite not knowing anything about the kana all have had a fantastic time.

However, if you're like me, you'll still want to learn a bit more before you go...

Japan has three alphabets – collectively called the kana: hiragana, katakana, and kanji.

Hiragana and katakana are so-called "syllabary alphabets" - each of the characters represents a single syllable. You have one character that represents the sound for "SU" and one character for "SHI" – and so すし is the hiragana for "sushi". Hiragana is used for spelling Japanese words as well as some more traditional concepts or ideas.

Meanwhile, the second syllabary alphabet, katakana, is used when spelling or adapting foreign words or English – on a visit to Tokyo you may see カラオケ (Ka-ra-o-ke) or コヒ (Ko-hi – Coffee).

Finally, Japanese also consists of more complicated single characters, which are really ideograms - called kanji – for instance, the kanji on the cover of this book, 酒, means "sake." There are thousands of such characters, and learning around 2000 kanji is often cited as the basic level for Japanese literacy.

If you have decided to visit Japan and to make the most of your time there, may I humbly suggest that you invest just a little bit of time to learn hiragana? A little effort will be well rewarded so that with a minor investment of time, your trip to Japan will be that much more meaningful. You may notice that a shop that sells delicious unagi has a gigantic and artful う (U) on the sign outside, or you also may start to recognize words and phrases that help you along your path to your favorite sake brewery in Japan.

There is an excellent book on this topic: *Remembering the Hiragana: A Complete Course on How to Teach Yourself the Japaneese Syllabary in 3 Hours* by James Heisig, that I suggest you seeking out.

Regionality in Sake

Inside Japan itself, the major sake producing regions of Japan certainly do have well-established regional styles. The obvious question is, how much does regionality or appellation apply to the sake you will taste? The simple answer is: not nearly so much as it does for wine.

Still, regional differences apply. As happens with other drink, beverages evolve to match regional cuisine. You can therefore expect sake from the mountain regions to go well with cured meats and hearty vegetables – the indigenous fare. Coastal areas with abundant fresh fish should have lighter, more delicate flavor so as not to overpower the local cuisine.

A seasoned sake expert, presented with blind tastings including representative sake from the various sake regions may not correctly identify the sake each time – or even half the time. Contrast this with a sommelier trying to distinguish Chanti from Burgundy. These "night and day" differences aren't expressed in sake.

If we were talking about wines - say, Italian and French wines – we might name the *very wine itself* by where the grapes are grown. The French Appellation d'origine contrôlée (AOC), Italian Denominazione di origine controllata (DOC) are on every bottle. These organizations set strictly enforced labeling rules. They even test wines to ensure that when a consumer buys a Champagne, it was actually made in Champagne.

Japan has recently taken steps to ensure that Japanese produced sake will be called Nihonshu -- that sake produced in other countries may not bear this stamp of premium quality and originality.

But in Japan and elsewhere, the sake you drink is legally defined by the grade; Futsushu, Aruten, Honjozo, Ginjo, Daiginjo, or Junmai. As I mentioned before, there are strict rules for these designations that rely on technical aspects of the sake and how it is made.

Nada in Kobe (Hyogo Prefecture) – Most of the large global sake brewers are located here in Nada, including Hakutsuru and Kikumasamune. Why does Nada have such a concentration of the big brewers? First, it's a port town, which means it has traditionally enjoyed easy transport to Tokyo. Second, Nada has plentiful water of a very high quality; a necessary and ideal attribute for the production of high quality sake. Nada sake is characterized by dryness and masculinity.

Fushimi in Kyoto – Another place with a fortunate concentration of plentiful and high quality water. Said to be softer and more feminine to Nada's masculine, Fushimi sake is generally slightly sweet and fragrant.

Niigata – We have established that water is an important part of sake regionality. This is also true for Niigata. The source of Niigata water? Snow. With abundant snow water, rice is also easily grown in the vicinity, and so Niigata terroir is firmly established. Niigata sake therefore is said to be clean, pure, and dry.

Akita – The two main components of sake production are rice and water – and Akita produces abundant rice and also gets its water from snowfall.

Hiroshima – Abundant and excellent water make Hiroshima sake soft and slightly sweet. Hiroshima is a historically important sake producer and is said to be the origin of Ginjo style premium sake.

Fukushima – Every batch of rice and water is hand tested by the government, so there is no reason to avoid Fukushima sake. In fact, helping the locals recover is an excellent reason to pursue this soft and light-as-air sake. Bring a bottle to a party and watch the conversation get interesting.

Shizuoka – Many sake have developed over time to complement the cuisine of the region, and Shizouka sake is light and goes well with fish.

Japan Travel Essentials

US Customs

Bringing Sake Back Home from Japan

The only thing better than enjoying sake where it is made is bringing some home with you to share as gifts. As it happens, you're in luck. Contrary to popular belief, there is NO LIMIT on the amount of sake you may bring back home with you (if you live in the USA). My advice is that you DECLARE ALL SAKE you bring back down to the drop. I don't want to hear that you've forfeited your sake to the border patrol.

No limits, within reason

As I am not a lawyer, nor a tax advisor, I would encourage you to double check my facts, but from the CFB website, there are no limits on the amount of alcohol, and therefore sake, you can bring back to the USA (readers from elsewhere, please check with your local authority).

From the USA CFB website:

> There is no federal limit on the amount of alcohol a traveler may import into the U.S. for personal use, however, large quantities might raise the suspicion that the importation is for commercial purposes, and a CBP officer could require the importer to obtain an Alcohol and Tobacco Tax and Trade Bureau (TTB) import license (which is required for all commercial importations) before releasing it. A general rule of thumb is that 1 case of alcohol is a personal use quantity - although travelers are still subject to state restrictions which may allow less. (https://help.cbp.gov)

So, if there is no limit, what gives?

The limits we read about are on "duty free" items. That is to say, you may bring 1 liter of alcohol per person without any duty (tax) applied and quantities greater than 1 liter incur a duty. I have read that the duty is 1% of the purchase price, and I have also found (on the CPB website) some ambiguous direction:

> Duty rates on alcoholic beverages are based on the percent of alcohol per liter in the product - not on units of packaging such as per bottle/case. Duty on wine and beer is generally low, $1-2 per liter, while fortified wines and spirits are considerably higher. Duty rates can be obtained in Chapter 22 "Beverages, Spirits and Vinegar," in the Harmonized Tariff Schedule. (http:// help.cpb.gov- Requirements for importing alcohol for personal use).

If asked, you may confidently provide guidance that sake is not "spirits and not liquor", and is made much more like beer and not distilled. Though I don't recommend arguing with agents, you may find the percentage of alcohol on the sake label, and it would be appropriate to point out that it is comparable to the strength of wine.

My advice is to therefore buy lots of sake in Japan, keep your receipts, and do as I do – bring an extra suitcase just for all the sake you're going to bring home, and proudly declare each and every drop.

I myself have regularly brought back 16-20 bottles of sake, and have never been levied the duty. However, I have also been told on several occasions that if I had not done so and the sake was found, they would have confiscated each and every bottle.

The real problem, therefore, is finding enough space for all of the delicious sake you're going to want to bring home with you.

I have personally discarded clothing and other items of value to make more room for sake on my trip home, but my advice simply to bring a empty duffel bag for soft items which you can pack and use as checked luggage on your return flight, leaving a roller or hard-sided suitcase for transporting your sake.

Japan Itinerary

So much sake, so little time! How to decide where to visit on your trip to Japan? To help you out I've listed my travel plans for Japan and when to go. Depending upon the length of your trip and intended number of stops, these would be my priorities. Rather than quick one-day stops to "see the things that need to be seen" in a mad rush, I prefer to linger at least for two nights, which increases the likelihood that you'll get to know a place a bit better and perhaps make some friends along the way.

3 days: Tokyo

5 days: Add Kyoto

7 days: Add Hiroshima

9 days: Add Hiroshima's Miyajima and Saijo

14 days: Add Osaka, Kobe, Nagano

21 days: Add Kochi

Note:
Arrivals from the US and Europe often land at Narita in the late afternoon or early evening – 3:00PM to 6:00PM Japan time. To make the most of your trip and to ease your entry into the new time zone, I suggest heading right into Tokyo. Check into your hotel, clean up, and then head out for the evening. Staying up as long as you can this first night will help you overcome jet lag and will set you up for the adventures ahead.

Jim's Best Three-Week Trip in Japan

Day 1:	Arrive at Tokyo's Narita Airport, connect to Tokyo via NEX or Airport Limousine (sleep in Tokyo)
Day 2:	Tokyo (sleep in Tokyo)
Day 3:	Tokyo (sleep in Tokyo)
Day 4:	Nagano (sleep Yudanaka)
Day 5:	Nagano (sleep Yudanaka)
Day 6:	Kyoto (sleep Kyoto)
Day 7:	Kyoto (sleep Kyoto)
Day 8:	Kyoto (sleep Kyoto)
Day 9:	Kyoto (sleep Kyoto)
Day 10:	Hiroshima (sleep Saijo)
Day 11:	Hiroshima (sleep Saijo)
Day 12:	Hiroshima (sleep Miyajima)
Day 13:	Kochi (sleep Kochi)
Day 14:	Kochi (sleep Kochi)
Day 15:	Kochi (sleep Kochi)
Day 16:	Kobe (sleep in Osaka or Kobe)
Day 17:	Kobe (sleep in Osaka or Kobe)
Day 18:	Osaka (sleep Osaka)
Day 19:	Osaka (sleep Osaka)
Day 20:	Tokyo (sleep in Tokyo)
Day 21:	Tokyo and departure from Narita!

By Shinkansen and Public Transportation

This three week itinerary is designed to be done by train. Traveling on Japan's famous "bullet trains" (shinkansen) is comfortable, efficient, cultural, and fun. I think traveling by train and experiencing how well the rail systems work is an important part of your visit. You'll find that the shinkansen, as well as the regional and local light rail systems, are immaculately clean, comfortable, economical, and always run on time.

When to Go

For Japan, peak travel seasons coincide with the winter break - December 26th to roughly January 6th when essentially everybody in Japan has vacation (and they all travel during this time – heading home for the holidays), and the cherry blossom season in late March and early April. Elaborate maps, forecasts, and real-time reports of the blooms make hanami (flower watching) a high-tech affair. Summer is a popular time to visit, but temperatures, humidity, and crowds soar.

I prefer visiting in shoulder season when temperatures and prices are both cooler. Visits in September, October, November, January, and February into early March are ideal. Fall and winter bring with them lower rates, wide open hotels, few crowds at sights, and no worries about weather. If you're a skier or snowboarder, you're in luck. Japan has more than 450 organized downhill slopes and some of the best snow in the world. Dress in layers and bring an umbrella.

My favorite visits have been in January and February. Sake brewers are all working, so you'll find the kuras open and workers busy, and will have the best shot at seeing something interesting. If you're lucky and can tour a working brewery, you might just enjoy the trip of a lifetime.

JR Rail Pass

When you travel to Japan, one of your top experiences will be riding one of the many wonderful trains. From the bustling JR Yamanote line circling the center of Tokyo to the elegant shinkansen connecting Japan's major cities, train travel in Japan is certainly "the way to go." I know I'm in Japan when I'm on a perfectly clean, quiet rail car being whisked away to my destination of choice.

When you visit Japan and follow any of my iteneraries, you will be riding aboard the "bullet train", or more properly called shinkansen. These train rides can be thought of more like flying - in terms of both price and speed. The trains travel at up to 200 miles per hour, and seats can be pricey - a ride from Tokyo to Kyoto ranges from about $100 to $150. On my favorite 7 day trip around Japan, purchasing rail tickets individually will quickly exceed $500. Purchasing a JR Rail Pass allows you to travel as much as you like in a 7 day period for $255.

If you can afford to splurge, the 7 day first class JR Rail Pass is $340 and is a worthwhile luxury.

Your JR Rail Pass also covers your travel on all JR lines during the activation period of your pass. This means that any travel in Kyoto or Tokyo - including ferries - are totally covered. So, if you're going to Japan you'll need to consider purchasing a JR Rail Pass.

JR Rail Passes are such a good deal that are only sold outside of Japan, and only to non-Japanese people. Do take advantage of this if it makes sense for your trip.

Important: you must activate your pass before starting to use it -- you need to have your passport with you when you activate, so don't forget it! JR Rail Passes can only be activated at certain train stations - Shibuya and Tokyo Station - and I would allow 1 hour or so total time to activate.

Don't plan on arriving at the train station at 1:00PM for a 2:00PM train - especially if you also plan on purchasing your eki-ben (bento box for train travel) before you board your shinkansen to be whisked away to the destination of your choice.

Money

The use of "electronic money" is both advanced and popular in Japan. The most obvious example are the access cards used on the trains and buses. These go by many brand names: JR East (Tokyo) issues a card called SUICA; JR West (Osaka/Kansai) calls their card ICOCA; the collective of private rail lines in Tokyo offers the PASSMO card – all of which are based on the FeliCa chip developed by Sony and are totally interchangeable throughout Japan. I suggest you get one as soon as you land at Narita.

When you purchase the card, you pay a small deposit (500 yen for SUICA) and the remainder of what you pay is used to "charge" the card. To use the card, simply place it over the scanner for a half-second until you hear a beep. The applicable fare or purchase price is deducted from the IC chip on the card (in the case of trains, the card also records where you entered the system and the balance of the fare, based on distance, will be deducted from the card when you exit). You can re-charge the card at most ticket machines.

However, don't forget to carry some cash!

Even though electronic banking is well-established in Japan, much of the economy still runs on a purely cash basis.

While major department stores, hotels, and restaurant chains accept most credit cards, cheques are pretty much non-existent, and smaller shops and restaurants are commonly cash-only. If you walk into a small restaurant or bar and don't see a credit card logo, the best bet is to verify up-front whether the establishment can accept credit card payment.

Important: almost none of the major Japanese banks support non-Japanese ATM networks, even if the ATM machines themselves have a button to display instructions in English. However, the ATM machines run by Japan Post (post offices) are connected to both the Cirrus and Plus networks and can also process credit card cash advances. If you're in need of some quick cash and your card was issued in the States, head to a post office instead of a bank.

Also be sure to plan your cash needs ahead of time. Banks in Japan keep traditional banker's hours and most close at 3pm on weekdays. Some branches in highly-trafficked areas such as Shinjuku will stay open later and some may even have limited hours on Saturday. But... basically... you should assume any banking that involves speaking to another human being will have to be done during normal business hours.

Moreover, don't assume the ATM machines are available 24/7. A few are (especially in the vicinity of larger train stations or at the airports) but most are not. They used to close when the bank closed but almost all bank branches have a separate area with ATM machines that stays open later. However, even these commonly close around 10pm, while post office ATMs close just before midnight on weekdays and around 9pm on weekends. If you get caught out partying at midnight on Sunday and run out of cash, you may well have a hard time replenishing your supply.

One of the ways to ensure your ability to buy a midnight snack, even if you run out of cash, is to keep your SUICA card charged up with at least a few thousand yen, as many 24-hour convenience stores accept SUICA payment.

Most cell phones sold in Japan (except the low-end phones) contain a FeliCa chip and can be used instead of a card. Often you will see commuters just scanning their phones over the ticket turnstyle as they enter and/or exit the train stations. Smart-phones, for example, come with an app which can be used to register the FeliCa chip in the phone with one or more of the electronic money networks. By associating the chip with a credit card, it becomes possible to re-charge the chip from just about anywhere without using cash.

Taxes:

Consider keeping your passport on you if you plan to do any shopping at all in Japan. You'll find the "duty free" option for foreigners saves you the 10% consumption tax in Japan.

Visitors to Japan are eligible to receive a refund of the consumption tax on most items when purchased, although not all shops offer the refunds. If you plan to make a major purchase, it would be best to do so in an area and shop frequented by tourists, and be sure to ask the sales clerk in advance whether that shop offers tax refunds (often called "duty free" in Japanese, even though the tax has nothing to do with duty). You must also spend over 10,000 yen in a single shop and present your passport to prove you're a tourist. Tax refunds are not available at the airport.

NEX and Airport Limousine

Getting to and from Tokyo

For economy and convenience, I fly in and out of Narita International Airport. Once there you have two very good options for getting into town: The ubiquitous orange busses called "Airport Limousine" and the speedy Narita Express train.

Airport Limousine

http://www.limousinebus.co.jp/en/

Airport Limousine operates an impossibly efficient bus system to whisk you back and forth from Narita Airport to many iconic Tokyo Hotels. The cost is about 3000 yen each way ($30, though you may find some discounts on the web. It is impossible to miss the bright orange ticket counter at Narita where you buy a ticket and take your bags 30 ft. more to the conductor, who will give you a receipt for each bag placed in the belly of the bus (keep these tickets, you'll need them). If you are looking for the smoothest possible entry into Japan, or if this is your first trip here I strongly recommend taking the Airport Limousine into town.

Choose your hotel

The Airport Limousine bus drops you off (and picks you up) at the following central Tokyo area hotels. If you can book your first night's stay at one of these hotels, your path into Japan will be very smooth indeed. Get off the plane, clear immigration, pick up your bags, exit and buy your Airport Limousine ticket telling them which hotel you're traveling to -- and you're there.

 Full disclosure: if you're taking a bus into the Tokyo core around rush hour (4pm-7pm), expect heavy traffic. It can take upwards of 2 hours to reach Shibuya station via the Airport Limousine. I've always been very happy to take a bus into Tokyo – you have the valuable opportunity to see the cityscape from above ground; views you don't get from the train.

Airport Limousine is perhaps the simplest way to reach Tokyo, and I recommend this to my friends and family visiting Japan for the first time. Get off your flight, buy a ticket, and you are whisked away to your hotel. Careful -- don't fall asleep and miss your stop once downtown.

Narita Express (NEX)

http://www.jreast.co.jp/e/nex/

The most time-efficient way to move from Narita International (Terminal 1 or 2) to Tokyo. After clearing immigration and collecting your bags, exit and follow the signs to NEX - you will head downstairs and know when you're getting close to a train station. You may ask the friendly information booths about where to purchase your NEX tickets, and I suggest going to a ticket counter.

No advance reservation is required except for 1st class cars, and though I can't imagine the airport being so busy as to cause you any problems, if you're traveling during the Olympics or another peak travel season, you may wish to make an advance purchase for Narita express to Tokyo and back on the JR East website.

The Narita Express (NEX) takes as little as 36 minutes for the express train and up to 55 minutes to reach Tokyo station. When you get ready to purchase your NEX ticket, note that the neighborhood and JR Yamanote line stop at which you're staying – the NEX has stops at Tokyo Station, Shinagawa, Shibuya, and Shinjuku, so if you're staying at any of these then no transfer will be necessary. If you're staying anywhere else, there will be the simple matter of transferring from NEX to the JR Yamanote line – all of which will be clearly marked in English.

Though completely unnecessary, combination locks are available for your use on the Narita Express trains – you can store your luggage there free from worry (and free of cost) of it being stolen. Perhaps if you have a ubiquitous black roller bag, you could lock it up in case it is mistaken for another.

My suggestion:

If you are traveling light and feel confident about your ability to negotiate train statuions in Europe, perhaps with a roller and a backpack like I suggest - take the NEX.

If you're worried about finding your way, or you are traveling with kids or want your entry to be particularly smooth, the Airport Limousine and one of the hotels on the list would be a wise choice for a first visit. As you gain confidence with JR and Japan rail systems, the NEX may make more sense. The airport limousine is also a total no brainer if you have a large roller of carrying your luggage is a burden.

Personally, I try to travel light and am always so eager to get straight downtown that I like the speed of NEX. No waiting, and downtown in 40 minutes. Yes, please!

Personal Technology in Japan

High speed internet and mobile connectivity for voice and text (and, yes, for your favorite social media ad mapping applications) is available everywhere you are likely to go in Japan. Increasingly, our domestic mobile providers are wise to the need for international access and are offering international roaming at much more reasonable rates than in the recent past. My plan on a major US carrier allows unlimited international calling, texting, and data for $10 each day it is used abroad. However, do check closely before you go -- roaming charges for data can add up quickly when you're sharing all of the amazing things you're going to see in Japan with friends back home. You don't want a surprise bill waiting for you upon your return so be careful - though I must say that the days when your vacation to Japan meant you'd be out of touch or that your personal technology would be unworkable are long gone.

I hear reports that pocket wifi and data roaming can be spotty in Europe. Not so in Japan -- you'll find your high speed internet really is just that, and you'll have all of the access you want. Of course, I caution you not to spend your valuable travel time with your nose pointed towards a mobile device!

Out of habit and seeking the best value, I usually ask my mobile provider to turn on a limited international data and calling plan, and also rent an unlimited local hot spot before leaving, using my phone's WiFi setting to ensure all of my data goes through the WiFi.

Arrange in advance via web reservation

You should arrange to rental a personal wifi device (sometimes called pocket wifi) in advance before you leave for Japan. I use a company called Global Advanced Communications (globaladvancedcomm.com), and since I'm a workaholic when I travel, particularly when I'm solo, I request the high speed pocket wifi which provides high speed access for my notebook computers and phones for the duration of my trip.

I'll usually order the wifi after making my first hotel reservation, and then I can note the hotel address on the wifi order. Without fail, the wifi has been waiting for me upon arrival at the hotel.

When the pocket wifi is delivered it is accompanied by a self-addressed courier mail envelope - so that on your last day, you can simply pop the pocket wifi into the envelope so it in a mailbox or with your hotel's front desk. There is also a post office at Narita in case you forget to mail it at the hotel (I speak from experience), or in case you'd like to use your wifi while waiting for your outbound flight.

<u>Arrange at airport</u>
You can also rent your pocket wifi right next to the Airport Limousine counter at Narita International Airport. You provide a credit card and pay your fee, and return the device upon your departure from Japan. This is a perfectly viable option if you forgot to arrange your access in advance.

I find that when I arrive in Narita, I want to get right on the bus or take the Narita Express into town and that I'm just a bit too tired or in too much of a hurry after a long flight to Japan to arrange for wifi.

This is obviously up to you, but I like to avoid frustration and complexity on my travel days.

Applications I find useful
<u>Hyperdia</u>
If you are planning on purchasing a JR pass for unlimited access to the shinkansen and JR lines, the Hyperdia app (published by Japan Railway itself) will help you find a route from wherever you are to wherever you're going using the extensive JR rail system - including shinkansen and local trains where your JR pass is valid.

I use the app to plot my course from one place to another, using it to tell me which combination of local trains or shinkansen I'm going to need.

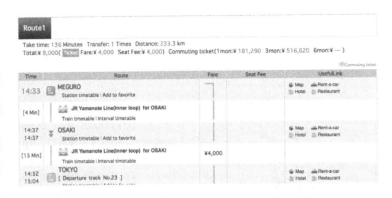

Time	Route	Fare	Seat Fee	UsefulLink
14:33	MEGURO Station timetable | Add to favorite			Map Rent-a-car Hotel Restaurant
[4 Min]	JR Yamanote Line(Inner loop) for OSAKI Train timetable | Interval timetable			
14:37 14:37	OSAKI Station timetable | Add to favorite			Map Rent-a-car Hotel Restaurant
[15 Min]	JR Yamanote Line(Inner loop) for OSAKI Train timetable | Interval timetable	¥4,000		
14:52 15:04	TOKYO [Departure track No.23]			Map Rent-a-car Hotel Restaurant

Google Maps

When first started traveling, Google Maps was not very helpful. It continues to improve. You may find that place names are in kanji and unreadable -- so, use the maps in this book!

I have mentioned that you should not worry about travel to Japan—that you will encounter English in many unexpected places. While this is true, there are times when Google Translate has come in quite handy indeed.

If you install the application on your mobile device, it will scan and translate both written and spoken language.

Since you'll have your pocket wifi with you, why let a little thing like language get in the way of complete enjoyment of your trip to Japan? Install Google Translate and find your language barrier melt away completely.

Tokyo

The city of Tokyo itself will be one of the top attractions you "see" when you visit Japan. It's the largest metropolitan city in the world and I'd venture to say the safest. From idyllic parks and temples to bustling train stations, Tokyo is a feast for the senses. Walking through Shibuya one night with Paul DeGraaf, a local big-shot and longtime resident of Tokyo, he asked me, "You see how 10 years can fly by just like THAT?" as he snapped his fingers. Certainly, Tokyo has a way of grabbing hold of you, sucking you in, and never letting go. When I'm in Tokyo, I can't help but imagine that I'm getting a lucky glimpse, or some sort of sneak preview of what the world will look like in the future.

Still, some may say that Tokyo is an assault on the senses. They don't like the loud hawkers and they feel that the marketing messages and bright lights are so much pollution. They say the people are unfriendly, and that here aren't any trash receptacles on the street. One of the biggest misperceptions, however, is that people think Japan and Tokyo are "too expensive."

Nonsense!

I spend four months out of every year traveling and Tokyo is among the most economical places I visit. You can find a fine, comfortable, safe room in a thoroughly interesting Tokyo neighborhood for the same price as a fleabag motel on the wrong side of the tracks in Sacramento, California. If you follow my advice, Tokyo can be a budget travel destination

The Yamanote Line

JR (Japan Rail) operates the Yamanote line, a circle line in central Tokyo. Known affectionately as "Yamanote-sen" by locals, a ride on the Yamanote is my favorite introduction to Tokyo and Japan. When you're in Tokyo I suggest acquainting yourself with Yamanote-sen --- you can travel quickly and economically to many of the important attractions in Tokyo.

My advice is that you obtain a SUICA card as soon as you get to Japan. It will make paying for your rides on the Yamanote pain-free. SUICA is a prepaid payment card that you can use all over Japan for paying for train and bus fares, as well as for other incidental expenses along the way. You'll see kiosks in almost every train station for the purchase of a SUICA card, and if you need help, it's never more than a mere button push away. Somebody may pop right out of the wall, literally, to help you out. After all, this is Japan we're talking about.

TOKYO

You'll notice that locals flip out their wallet or other card carrier and just wave it by the turnstile – you hear a beep and the turnstile flies open. When you arrive at your destination, wave your SUICA by the turnstile again and your fare will be deducted from your card, with the value remaining displayed on a little digital readout. You can use your SUICA almost everywhere trains go in Japan – once you get out into the mountain or onto smaller rail lines you may have to purchase individual tickets, but the small investment in time and energy to obtain a SUICA when you land in Narita or as soon as you arrive in Tokyo is certainly worthwhile.

You can buy your SUICA card upon arrival at the JR Narita train station. Depending upon my schedule, I usually pop down there and recharge my SUICA before my scheduled Airport Limousine or Narita Express ride into town.

Meguro

When I'm exploring a new city, or coming back to one I love, I always try to stay and live like a local – and Tokyo is no exception. There are some wonderful neighborhoods to visit – Roppongi, Shibuya and Shinjuku come to mind – and these are all bustling, fast-paced places that remind me of Times Square in New York or Champs Elysee in Paris. I to want visit these places to explore, but I'd prefer to pop in on the train – and then pop right back out again to my "happy place" at the end of the day. Don't get me wrong – Times Square and Champs Elysees are wonderful places to visit and they have some lavish hotels – but if I'm maximizing value and time, I stay a couple of train stops away. You spend far less and get more traveling like a local.

When in Tokyo, Meguro is my home base. I find that it is "just enough" of Tokyo – I can wander around here comfortably and see amazing and new things – but also easily pop in to a neighborhood grocery store.

As much as I can, I like to see and do and live as a temporary local when I travel, and if you're like me, you're going to want to stay in Meguro.

TOKYO

TOKYO

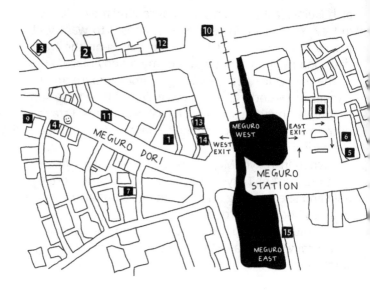

As you arrive at Meguro station on the Yamanote line and exit the turnstile (using your new SUICA card to pay as you leave the station) look for a sign indicating "East Exit" or "West Exit" and try to get yourself oriented. If you exit and see **5** 31 Flavors and **6** McDonalds, you'll know you are at the East Exit. If you look out and see a bus stop and across the street **13** Yoshinoya and a **14** flower shop, you will be at the West Exit. Buy some flowers there at the flower shop and head on down the hill.

As you head downhill, you may decide to stay at **1** Hotel Abest Meguro which is an excellent value and one of my regular spots. It is a bit older, but has spacious rooms by Japanese standards with thick walls and with good electrical outlets, free WIFI, and a decent Japanese style breakfast buffet each morning which I find convenient. I also frequent **4** Hotel Mid in Meguro which is newer and sits above a Starbucks. It's a bit fancier and if you won't have time for breakfast, or prefer a quick coffee downstairs at Starbucks you might decide to stay here over Abest Meguro. If you're looking to save even more money, consider **2** Hotel Wing and **3** Hotel Verdure though also not fancy, they are comfortable and put you in Meguro with the many shops, convenience stores, markets, izakaya, and close to the train station which is a key benefit.

1 HOTEL ABEST MEGURO

2 HOTEL WING INTERNATIONAL

3 HOTEL VERDURE

4 HOTEL MID IN MEGURO EKIMAE & STARBUCKS

5 "31 FLAVORS" ICE CREAM

6 MCDONALDS MEGURO EKIMAE

7 TONKI

8 MORIVA COFFEE

9 "7-11" CONVENIENCE STORE

10 MOS BURGER

11 FUON WA BISTORO SAKE BAR

12 MEGURO CINEMA

13 YOSHINOYA

14 FLOWER SHOP

15 TULLY'S COFFEE

TOKYO

A local favorite and "must do" when in Meguro is **7** Tonki a Katsu restaurant which serves pork katsu, fried pork cutlets with shredded cabbage and addictive sauces, with moderately priced set price meals and – the food here is plentiful and absolutely delicious. This is an example of very approachable food that will delight the picky eaters, and also surprise those who view Japan as a place with only "raw fish." A great sake spot is **11** Fuon Wa Sake bar which is decorated entirely with sake swag. Familiar to those back home in name only is Yoshinoya **13** which I feel is actually worth a visit. Budget meals which are delicious and economical. Healthy by American standards, you may find Japanese people think a bowl of rice and beef with a few vegetables is "junk food." Personally, a $5 breakfast or lunch that hits the spot, and with menus that have lots of pictures – "If you can point, you can eat..."

A good orientation: Exit Meguro station using the West Exit. Walk down the hill veering slightly left so you can pass Hotel Abest, Hotel Mid and Starbucks. Stop in at **9** 7-11 to grab a green tea, and continue walking downhill until you reach the Meguro River. Pop into a grocery store or ramen shop along the way and make a friend. Meguro is that kind of place. Make a right at the River and explore the trendy and charming Naka Meguro neighborhood. Get lost. Explore.

Tokyo
Breweries

Aiyu Sake Brewery

205, Tuji Itako City, Ibaraki, Japan 311-2421
http://www.aiyu-sake.jp/
📱 Shop +81-299-62-2234 📠 Fax +81299622250
🕐 Shop daily 8am - 5pm Touring closed Nov-Feb
🚆 JR Kashima - Itako / Bus - Itako

How to get there:

There are a few different ways to reach Aiyu Sake. If you plan
to visit, try to call ahead first – the generous and wonderful
Kanehiras, who run the Aiyu Sake Brewery in Itako City, can arrange to pick you up at Itako station. When in Tokyo, I suggest
you set aside the afternoon, and I have no doubt you will agree
that any little bit of extra effort you expend to visit Aiyu is completely warranted. You won't regret visiting this brewery.

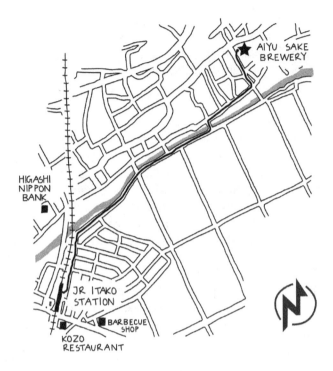

Train: Cheapest but will take roughly an hour and a half.

Bus: More expensive than train and will take around 40 minutes.

Take the JR Kashima line located between Itako and Narita. Once you reach Itako City, begin at JR Itako train station.

If you're going by bus, don't fall asleep and miss your stop! You will likely be dropped at the Itako train station, and you may then follow the directions below.

Driving to the brewery from Itako station takes roughly 5 minutes and walking may take you about a half and hour. After walking, the Kanehiras insisted that I should have called from the station and that they would have gladly given me a ride.

In any case, from the station, head north on the street parallel to the east side of the station. Proceed to the river. After you have crossed the river, continue two more streets north then make a right onto roadway 5. You will know you reach this road when you see a building on your left with a big red sign that has an S on it. From here, continue west on roadway 5 for about eight streets and follow it as it turns left, then right. Continue down another 4 streets and you will reach a shrine. Take this street right and the Aiyu brewery will be on either side of you.

The Brewery:

The facilities are in a couple of different buildings - the brewery, the shop, the office, and the bottling plant. When you first arrive, head to the shop. This will be the entrance on your left from the main road. Once here, talk to someone to help you get started with a tour or answer any questions you may have. Aiyu is a modern day "semi-local" brewery. This means Aiyu supplies much of what it produces to locals – people living in surrounding cities. It means they produce some really excellent sake by any standard.

On the tour you will be able to see the brewery in its entirety as your guide explains the process used to craft the fine sake they sell. Afterward, you may sample several varieties of sake. The owner's daughter who helps run the place speaks a little English. When calling to make reservations, you can ask to be picked up from the JR Itako station. This is not an imposition, particularly if you schedule your visit in advance by making a reservation. Aiyu is open to bending some of its rules to help facilitate brewery tours and they may stay open later to give you a tour - so don't be afraid to call and ask!

History:

The Aiyu sake brewery was established roughly 200 years ago in 1804. It has been in the Kanehira family since opening, the senior member currently being Michiko Kanehira. Her daughter Rikako is next in line to take over the business when her mother decides to retire. Aiyu firmly believes that the popularity and taste of their sake stem from the quality of the water used in the sake brewing process. In addition, the application of knowledge and experience of their most senior toji ensures that all the correct brewing steps are followed. Up until recently, Aiyu's toji (brewmaster) was a man named Abe-san. Now it is a man named Tada-san. Both men are dedicated individuals that have given their life's work to the art of crafting premium sake. Just as Abe-san once gave 20 or so years of his life to this brewery, Tada san will probably want to do the same.

Final Thoughts:

The Aiyu sake brewery in Itako City is a fun place to visit in its own right, but the Kanehiras – these people are the heart of the brewery and what makes visiting it such a worthy endeavor. If you can make the trip, a lifetime of fond memories and perhaps a few new friends for life will be your reward. Being welcomed to this brewery as I was, with such hospitality and generosity, is something you will never forget.

TOKYO

Ishikawa Brewery

1 Kumagawa, Fussa City, Tokyo 197–8623, Japan
http://www.tamajiman.com/english/index.html
📱 Shop +042-553-0100 📱 Fax +042-553-2017
E-mail: liveinfo@tamajiman.co.jp
🕐 Shop daily 10am - 6pm Touring closed Nov-Feb
🚃 JR Seibu Haijima - Haijima

How to get there:

The easiest way to get to Ishikawa brewery is to start by exiting at Haijima station from either JR Hachiko line, JR Itsukaichi
line, or JR Ome line. From here, start by going west on roadway 164 - it will take you to roadway 16. Stay straight on 164
through 16 and now roadway 16 will have turned into roadway 7. If you are walking, continue on the left hand side of

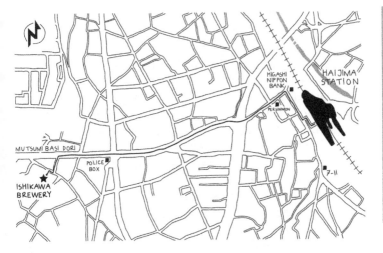

the street. Keep going straight and you will reach roadway 29, which is also written in English as "Okutama Highway." Continue straight through Okutama and continue down about three more streets before making a left turn. You will then have reached the street that takes you outside the brewery. Follow the turn up the hill a little and continue straight down the street. In roughly 400-500 yards you will see the entrance to the brewery. Make a right and on the left hand side will be parking while on the right is the main entrance. Please go to the front desk from here for further assistance.

The Brewery:

The Ishikawa sake brewery and surrounding area in Fussa City is a very beautiful and ultimately very historical place. But unlike your visits to the more popular and heavily visited areas of Japan, when you visit this brewery you feel that you are somehow now a part of that history. The brewery is broken up among several buildings; the brewing facilities, the bottling plant, the store, and the restaurants. There are two restaurants here – a traditional Japanese and an Italian restaurant. Above the restaurants you will also find a small museum dedicated to the history of the Ishikawa sake brewery. Linking all buildings is a beautiful garden that compliments the traditional (and gorgeous) style of architecture you'll see at Ishikawa. Sit here in the garden among the many trees and taste a sake or two.

As you might expect, the store offers every variety of sake made at the brewery as well as the beer they have on tap. I had a particularly hard time saying no to the many sake related souvenirs available. The front desk is where a tour may be requested. The tour covers most of the facilities on the premises, including very interesting artifacts from the early Meiji era. On the tour you will hear the full history of the Ishikawa brewery as well as see most of the machinery they use to brew sake year round. The story of a massive brewing kettle and how it survived the war is particularly intriguing. After the tour you can sample a few different varieties of sake or beer. The restaurant is open year-round and you might try some soba paired with one of the delicious Ishikawa sake. There is also an Italian restaurant here and if you need a break from traditional Japanese fare, a pizza might hit the spot. Ultimately, I hope you agree with my assessment that sake tastes best when you drink it close to where it is made. You'll find that applies doubly here in Fussa City and at the Ishikawa sake brewery.

History:

The original brewery was built in 1863 and has been held in the Ishikawa family since opening. The brewery has survived all of the ups and downs of the sake industry and the war. Currently lead by Taro Ishikawa, the brewery continues to build upon the rich tradition of sake while also embracing modern production techniques and trends, and is currently producing several premium sake. Initially, Ishikawa began production of sake and later moved to producing both sake and beer in the late 1880's. Since the founding of the brewery, Ishikawa has gone through a few name changes but the brewery has always been owned by the same family. At Ishikawa they believe strongly that the correct choice of water for a brewing process has a direct impact on the overall quality of the sake. This is why Ishikawa takes pride in using mineral well water for all brewing at this facility.

Final Thoughts:

Fussa city is just 40 minutes by train from Tokyo. It is a great little suburb with lots of culture, and the brewery is located close to the hills near abundant natural spring water. This is a fantastic brewery to visit if you need a break from the hustle and bustle of the city. If you have limited time in Japan and only have the major cities on your itinerary, visiting a suburb like Fussa should be a priority. You'll learn much about "real Japan" and will have a real chance of making some friends along the way. It is very peaceful here but there is always something to do - a great place to spend half a day. All the staff I've met here are very friendly, and assure me that my readers are most welcome and can tour the facilities any time of year.

TOKYO

Nakagawa Shuzo Brewery

1875 Kanagawa Ashigarakami, Matsuda Matsudasoryo, Japan 258-0003

📱 Shop +0465-82-0024 📱 Fax +0465-83-5332

🕐 Shop daily 10am - 5pm Touring closed Nov-Feb

🚆 Odakyu Shin-Matsuda

How to get there:

One of the easiest ways to reach Nakagawa Shuzo is via the Odakyu line, otherwise known as the Odakyu Electric Railway or OER. This line runs between the city of Odawara (just outside of Tokyo) and Shinjuku station in Tokyo. Please check your favorite train schedule or route-finding app – you will have many options to reach Odakyu Shin-Matsuda. From Shin-Matsuda station, take the north exit then make an immediate left. This leads to a parking lot. Continue straight about one hundred feet to the street in front of you and then turn left. Follow this street down five blocks, passing the Bank of Yokohama on your left. Continue past the Wakamatsu Canteen and the Charcoal BBQ Chicken restaurant on your

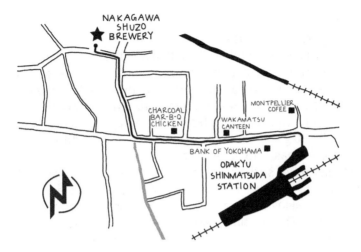

right until you reach a small dry goods store, also on your right. Take the street to the right once you reach this corner. If you reach the Sunkus convenience store you have gone too far. Continue straight down this street and take the first left. The brewery will be to your right while the sake shop will be on your left.

The Brewery:

The facilities are split up among the brewery and the sake shop across the street. Nakagawa Shuzo is small and family owned, and this is one of the brewery's greatest strengths. You'll make friends here. The brewery tours are generally pretty quick and they will explain in much detail the full process they go through when making sake at Nakagawa Shuzo. They cater to English speaking-customers, and the fact that they craft their sake by hand is very noticeable, with the rich history of Nakagawa Shuzo written all over the walls inside. Across the street is a shop where all varieties of sake in production can be purchased. Here you will also find a video available in English as well as Japanese on the subtleties of sake production and the impact that water has on the sake brewing process. You will be able to taste all of the sake they have here free of charge.

History:

Nakagawa Shuzo was established in 1825 by the Akira family. The most senior member of the family at the moment is Shigeru Akira who is, remarkably, also the current toji. He is getting ready to retire soon and has been training his son, Kagiwada Akira, to take over as toji. Interesting fact: not only is the young Akira-san a master toji in his own right, but he is also a sake scientist. Kagiwada is currently experimenting with extracting tastes, aromas, and other aesthetic qualities from fruits, flowers, and other such things to add to the sake. It is Kagiwada's mission to discover new and interesting varieties and methods for making Nakagawa Shuzo's products better and more enjoyable. The last time I visited he was able to let me sample some of the rose bud sake he has been developing. This is not available to the general public, but you should ask to try some of his experimental sake – it is all delicious.

I am supremely confident that Akira-san will soon make a breakthrough with one of his experiments and find something he likes. When he does, people all over the world will certainly know about it.

Final Thoughts:

Nakagawa Shuzo is a special place. I love this quiet area of town - it amplifies the close family presence you feel when you visit this brewery. The Akira family will work to ensure you are comfortable and will insist on providing for you if you need anything at all. All of your questions will be answered on the spot about all subjects, even if you ask about their secret recipe (they do not have one). If love and affection translate at all into a family's work, nowhere is it easier to find than right here at Nakagawa Shuzo.

After the tour when I was able to sit down and sample all the sake they offer, Akira-san made sure to tell me the history of a few sake they regularly stock. They have been producing several of the same sake for years due to their popularity. Akira-san also provided some tips on the best temperatures, foods, and even times of day when their sake can be enjoyed to its fullest potential. Not only do they make great sake at

Nakagawa Shuzo, they are also passionate about what they do. The Akiras love educating and informing the public that their sake is not necessarily better but just different. A visit to Nakagawa Shuzo is in a class all on its own – it will be hard for you to find a warmer, more delightful place to visit in Tokyo. Nakagawa Shuzo should therefore be considered a pilgrimage for any sake enthusiast looking to find hand-crafted premium sake in the greater Tokyo area.

Tokyo Sake Pubs

Many of my readers will find themselves planning a 7 or 10 day journey in Japan. If, despite your best efforts, you find yourself unable to visit a kura (sake brewery) while you're in Tokyo, perhaps you can take a quick spin over to one of my favorite sake pubs instead. Here is a smattering in order of preference:

SASAGIN
1F Dai Ni Kobayashi Biru
1-32-15 Yoyogi Uehara
Shibuya-ku, Tokyo
Open 5pm to 11:30pm, on Saturday from 5pm to 11pm. Closed Sunday and national holidays.

Yoyogi-uehara station (Odakyu Odawara and Chuyoda lines) Exit South 1. Turn right. It is less than 100 yards on your left. Moderate prices. 80-90 sake. Constantly turns up on top 10 food and sake experience lists.

AKAONI
www.akaoni39.com
2-15-3 Sangenjaya, Setagaya-ku, Tokyo

One of the best known premium sake pubs in Tokyo. Open since 1982.
    Sengenjaya station (Tokyu Denentoshi line). Exit the central gates of Sengenjaya station and take the North Exit. Walk straight ahead across the side road, then cross the main road

to Big Echo Karaoke. Bear right toward the Carrot Tower. Go left just after the bicycle park, right at the T-junction and right again at the end of the block beside the car park.

TAKARA
B1F Tokyo International Forum
3-5-1 Marunouchi
Chiyoda-ku, Tokyo 1000-0005

Yurakucho station underground concourse, exit D5. Go straight ahead into the Tokyo International Forum. Takara is on your left, immediately after the big orange sign to "Hall C".

On the forefront of introducing premium sake to foreigners, and a good place to start if you want to learn more about sake. Tapas-inspired menu.

Kyoto

While Tokyo offers you a glimpse into the future, Kyoto reveals a rich past. Young couples amble in kimono, and wandering a lantern-lined street after dark really give Kyoto a special feel. The political (and therefore cultural) capital of Japan for 1000 years, Kyoto was spared bombing at the end of World War II – more history - and therefore the temples, shrines, and gardens here are not to be missed.

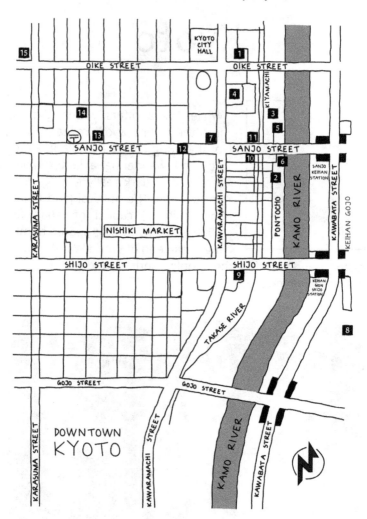

The area surrounding **2** **Pontocho street called "Sanjo"** or also "Downtown" or "Central" Kyoto is one of my favorite neighborhoods in Japan, and everyone I've sent here has agreed. Not far from the Westin Miyako, Pontocho is a traditional narrow wood-lined pedestrian walkway with plenty of dining choices. It is particularly charming at night with the lanterns glowing; it is a good place to follow your nose and perhaps find your favorite meal in Japan.

Downtown Kyoto & Sanjo Sanjo

1 HOTEL OKURA
2 PONTOCHO STREET
3 SAMA SAMA
4 KYOTO PALACE HOTEL
5 STARBUCKS
6 LAWSON
7 MUSASHI SUSHI
8 GION
9 MC DONALDS
10 BURGER KING
11 ROYAL PARK HOTEL
12 SANJO SHOPPING ARCADE
13 KYOTO MUSEUM
14 KYOTO KALEIDOSCOPE MUSEUM
15 KYOTO INTERNATIONAL MANGA MUSEUM

During the day, nearby Nishiki market and **12 Sanjo shopping arcade** is a massive food and sundry market. Highly conducive to unstructured exploration and to see the sights, sounds, smells of Kyoto. You can also purchase a hand- made wooden comb (static-free), or some Japanese steel (right and left hand-ed); two things of beauty you'll find nowhere else in the world.

1 Kyoto Hotel Okura 3 Sama Sama – great little bar whose owner speaks English, a nice guy, who taught me about Japan real estate and business taxes **4 Kyoto Palace Hotel 5 Starbucks**

6 Lawson Convenience Store 7 Musashi sushi is a kaiten zushi restaurant where the sushi dance along by on a convey-or belt. Take what you like, and watch the rest. Extremely fresh and busy – you'll never see the same piece of fish go by twice. For some reason strangers seem to become friends here. If you want something special, call it out to the chef and he'll make to order. At about $1.50 for each plate, and with free green tea, this is a great value. Perhaps a place to rest after exploring Nishiki market.

8 Gion 9 McDonalds – use as geographical reference only, please!

10 Burger King 11 Royal Park Hotel 13 Kyoto Museum

14 Kyoto Kaleidoscope Museum 15 Kyoto International Manga Museum

Jim's Favorites in Kyoto

Kyoto's Good Samaritan Club Schedule a tour with a local university student. The Japanese students appreciate any chance to practice their English, and you get a free tour of your choice in Kyoto. You buy lunch or dinner, and potentially make a friend for life. My tour guides have become friends over the years and I rate a tour with a Good Samaritan in Kyoto as a top Japan experience.
http://www.geocities.jp/goodsamaritanclub_hp/

UNIQLO Pick up a sharp new ultra light-weight and compact jacket at UNIQLO on Kawaramachi street. UNIQLO has just opened in New York, and I believe will inevitably become a dominant global brand. Get yours first, right at the source. Also at The Ginza in Tokyo.

Fushimi Inari Taisha Wander through the gorgeous bright orange prayer gates (torii) and pay tribute to the god of the rice harvest and his/her fox messengers.

Arashiyama Get lost in the bamboo forest – and take lots of pictures.

Ninnaji, Ryoanji, Kinkakuji My favorite temples in Kyoto. Map attached. Highly efficient to visit in that order and walk between each temple. A very nice morning or afternoon excursion.

Ryoanji's famous rocks are worth visiting, but the tofu restaurant tucked way back in the botanical garden may change your life.

Day trip to Nara visit the famous deer of Nara and feed them some "deer cookies" – then visit the largest and oldest wooden temple in Japan and see the big Daibutsu there. Climb through "his nose" and be granted enlightenment.

Kyoto
Breweries

KYOTO

Gekkeikan Okura Sake Museum

247 Minami-cho, Fushimi-ku, Kyoto 612-8660
http://www.gekkeikan.co.jp/english/
Shop +075-623-2056 Fax +075-621-7571
Shop daily 9:30am-4:30pm closed O-Bon and New Years holidays
Keihan Fushimimomoyama (Fu-shi-mi-mo-mo-ya-ma)

How to get there:

The easiest way to reach the Gekkeikan Okura Sake Museum is via the Keihan Main Line, otherwise known as the Keihan Electric Railway, which runs between Sanjo station in Kyoto and Yodoyabashi station in Osaka. Start by exiting at Fushimimomoyama station. From here, walk west through a covered outdoor shopping mall. You will then take the second left at the Mizuho bank. If you pass a 7-11 then you have gone too far. After this left walk to the end of the street. You will approach a T intersection - follow it to the right and then around the corner to the left. Then proceed straight until the end of the street. The sake museum will be on your right.

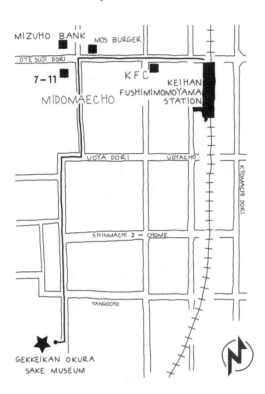

History:

Gekkeikan is located in the center of the old Fushimi district in Kyoto. Here the natural spring water that flows beneath the ground is prized for its softness and delicate taste. Both are qualities that define the regional characteristics of this important sake producing region in Japan. Gekkeikan was established in 1637 by founder Jeimon Okura. The brewery has been in the Okura family since opening with its most senior member right now being Haruhiko Okura. During the early years of operation, the brewery saw great success in their manufacturing of sake due to much trade between Osaka and Edo, as well as the love of most of Kyoto's inhabitants. In the late 1800s, the brewery started seeing more competitors pop up all over Japan and needed to devise ways to stay ahead of the game–so the brewers opened a separate and private research facility to test new ways of improving production of sake. The brewers at Gekkiekan were thus among the first in Kyoto to use machines and electricity to help speed along the sake production process. Later into the mid 1900's, Gekkeikan wanted to grow and spread the love of sake all over the world, and so decided to set up another brewery in the U.S.A. If you happen to be in Sacramento, California, Gekkikan USA's brewery in Folsom is about a half hour drive from downtown. The next time you see sake at your local market, I'm sure there will be several from the kura Gekkikan. They're a top global producer.

The Brewery:

The museum you see here today is a replica of the original brewery that once sat at this location. The modern production brewery has, of course, been moved a few blocks down the street. A ¥300 fee will cover the museum's admission fee and you'll receive a small souvenir bottle of sake. As you proceed through the tour you will have the opportunity to taste some of the natural spring water they use to make Gekkeikan sake and will also see the tools used in the sake making process.

When you take the brewery tour, you will hear a recording of the sounds and songs of the old sake brewery. This is more of a world-class museum than a working brewery, and is a worthy place to visit. At the end of the tour you will also be able to sample 4-5 different varieties of Gekkikan sake. After tasting the sake, check out all the things they have for sale in their shop. You'll understand why I always find it impossible to resist picking up gifts for my friends back home.

Using real glasses, taste the "sakamizu", or prospering water. It is said if you taste the water here at Gekkikan in Fushimi, your destiny is be to become a lifelong lover of sake.

Final Thoughts:

Gekkeikan should be a top priority on your visit to Kyoto. The brewers and the Okura family have several centuries of sake making history to share and are very accommodating to people from all countries. Most of the staff speak English. Although it is one of the few museums that charge for admission, it is well worth the $3 with the gift bottle of sake you receive. Gekkeikan is one of the world's largest sake producers and it is a brand with which you should be familiar. The site is located in the old part of the Fushimi district in Kyoto, and finding your way here is an experience that itself is well worth the effort.

Kizakura Kappa Country

Shioya-chō 228 Fushimi-ku, Kyoto Japan
http://www.kizakura.co.jp/ja/en/index.html
📱 Shop +075 611 9919 ⊙ Shop Mon-Fri 11am-2pm & 5pm-9pm,
Sat-Sun 11am-10pm 🚆 Keihan - Fushimimomoyama

How to get there:

Your journey to the Kizakura Kappa Country sake brewery
starts at the familiar Fushimimomoyama station on the Keihan
line in Kyoto. From here, walk west through a covered outdoor
shopping mall. Take the second left at the Mizuho bank. If you
pass 7-11 you have gone too far. After you take this left walk to
the end of the street. You will approach a T intersection. Follow
the street to the right and around the corner to the left.

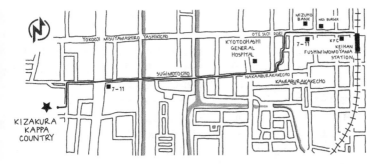

After following this street to the left, walk to the second street leading to the right. Walk down this street roughly half a block and Kizakura Kappa Country will be on both your right and left. The main building is on the right.

The Brewery:

The facilities you will visit are on the site of the old brewery. In the main building you will find a small museum featuring many old Kizakura Kappa commercials, some dating from the early 1920's all the way through today. In this side of the facility you will also find a sake shop as well as a restaurant. At this shop you may sample the sake – simply ask and you can taste anything you like. Because the production brewery is close by, they are able to sell nama, or unpasteurized sake, at this establishment. Give it a try!

Kizakura carries about half a dozen varieties of sake as well as their own versions of umeshu (plum wine) and citrus-infused sake. You can also find plenty of small gifts such as shirts, keychains, and sake ware at the shop. The rest of the sake museum is on the opposite side of the street. There you can see original bottles and labels that have been kept around for posterity. There are many interesting facts printed on the walls and small displays that go over the sake brewing process. Look for a window right into the production facility where you can watch the last step in brewing: pressing the moto into delicious sake.

KYOTO

History:

Kizakura Kappa Country has been run by the Matsumoto family since opening, with the most senior member currently being Shinji Matsumoto. The brewery at Kizakura Kappa Country was built during the Taisho period - sometime between the years 1912 and 1926. It is one of the newer breweries in the Fushimi area (hard not to be the new kid on the block with nearby breweries founded in the 1600s!) but has made a big name for itself by being the first to try many new marketing ideas. They were among the first brewers to use commercials as well as give free samples to customers to boost sales. Although Kizakura Kappa Country has not been around as long as some of its competitors, it is obvious that they have earned a place among the great sake breweries of Fushimi.

Final Thoughts:

The staff here are very friendly and ready to answer any questions you might have. The restaurant is excellent, and you may find it surprisingly full. Kizakura Kappa Country is a great place to take a break from the hustle and bustle of touring around and seeing all that Kyoto has to offer. If you want to grab a quick bite, or just want to be in a traditional setting of Kyoto, look no further than Kizakura Kappa Country.

*Two old friends enjoying each other's
company over a sake at
Kyoto's Otagi Nenbutsuji.*

Yamamoto Honke

36-1 Kamiaburakake-cho, Fushimi-ku, Kyoto 612-8047
http://www.kyotosake.com/index.html
📱 Shop +81-75-611-0211 📱 Fax +81-3-3761-1737 ⊙ Shop
daily 10am-5pm Tours close Nov-Jan 🚆 Keihan Fushimimomoyama (Fu-shi-mi-mo-mo-ya-ma){insert Kyoto/yamomoto honke.png}

How to get there:

The easiest route to the Yamamoto Honke sake brewery is
from the Keihan line. Start by exiting the train at Fushimimomoyama station. As you exit the station you will walk west
through a covered outdoor shopping mall called Otesuji. Take

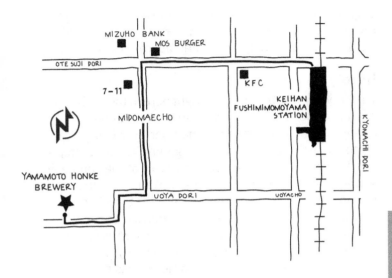

the second left at the Mizuho bank. The bank will be on your right. If you pass the 7-11 you have gone too far. After taking this left, walk to the end of the street. At the end of the street, head right and around the corner to the left. Then proceed a hundred or so feet down this road and you will approach the shop and restaurant. The brewery is split up among three buildings in various locations, all close to the shop and restaurant.

The Brewery:

The staff are very friendly here and easily accommodate English speaking visitors. Most of the facilities are available for touring, particularly if reservations are made in advance. Simply navigate over to the website and let them know you're coming – a courtesy that will go a long way in Japan. The facilities also include a shop and restaurant. The shop accommodates all of the 7 or 8 varieties of sake made at Yamamoto Honke as well as some of their own "fresh" draft sake. The restaurant, no kidding, boasts some of the best food in Kyoto. This brewery has been on the same plot of land since it opened, and has forgone moving to new locations for facilities upgrades to instead be upgraded in place. The owners told me that they didn't feel like moving because the place they were at was home. Yamamoto Honke has been family owned and operated since opening.

History:

The brewery was built in 1677, right here in the Fushimi district of Kyoto. The brewery has been in the Yamamoto family since opening, with its most senior member now being Koji Yamamoto (though Yamamoto-san is getting ready to step down and his son will soon take over as head of the company). His son will mark the 12th generation of Yamamoto to run the Yamamoto Honke brewery. The brewery has been knocked down by wars and earthquakes - literally burned to the ground by fire over the years - yet each time the brewery is reconstructed by the family, with assistance from the many locals who know and love the sake that Yamamoto Honke has crafted over the years. Yamamoto Honke has won many prestigious awards for their sake and have been slowly gaining greater influence over all of Japan. They have also recently started distributing their sake internationally. Check out Yamamoto Honke's website for more details and to make a reservation for a tour of the brewery.

Final Thoughts:

Yamamoto Honke is one of my favorite breweries in Kyoto for a reason. It's hard to explain, but a very familiar family feeling pervades this brewery. You just feel at home when you're visiting, touring, and tasting the sake they craft here. Everyone on the staff is extremely gracious and will assist you with any questions or concerns you may have. Not all of them speak English but they will certainly find someone to assist should you need any help. It has been a family establishment ever since its founding, and when you walk into their home they immediately make you feel welcome and at ease. When touring the brewery, not only do you get to see how things used to be done but also how the brewing process is done today. Tastings for almost everything they sell are available after the tour, which is a great way to start a first class meal in their restaurant. Yamamoto Honke has a small spring outside of their store where they allow you to fill up on the softest spring water in all of Japan... for free!

Before leaving the brewery, Yamamoto-san told me, "We are all family here!" and I genuinely believe that. So when you're in Kyoto, don't miss visiting your new family here: the brewers at Yamamoto Honke.

KYOTO

Kobe

Nestled between the Rokko mountains and beautiful Osaka bay is the city of Kobe. Kobe is Japan's sixth largest city with about 1.5 million residents and is the capital of Hyogo prefecture. It is also home to one of the most important sake producing regions in all of Japan: Nada.

Kobe is also a mere 18 miles away from Osaka – very close by – so if you find yourself in Kyoto or Osaka, a trip to the sake breweries of Nada in Kobe should be very high on your list of priorities. Nowhere else can you so quickly and effectively gain such a sense of Japanese culture and possibly make a new friend or two on your trip to Japan.

The climate in Kobe is said to produce some of the best rice in all of Japan (Yamada Nishiki) which is essential for brewing quality sake. The coupling of the brewing process with natural spring water from the Rokko Mountains (miyamizu) creates a brew for which only the Nada area is known.

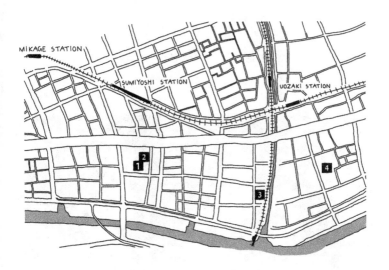

MIKAGE STATION
SUMIYOSHI STATION
UOZAKI STATION

1 HAKUTSURU   SAKE MUSEUM
2 HAMAFUKUTSURU SAKE BREWERY
3 KIKUMASUMUNE SAKE MUSEUM
4 SAKURAMASAMUNE SAKURAEN

When you visit sake breweries in Japan,

expect to make a new friend along the way.

Kobe Breweries

Hakutsuru Sake Museum

4-5-5 Sumiyoshi Minami-machi, Higashinada-ku, Kobe, Hyogo, Japan 658-0041

http://www.hakutsuru.co.jp/english/

📱 Shop +078-822-8907 📠 Fax +078-822-4891

🕐 **Shop daily 9:30AM-4:30PM closed Bon - Festivals, New Years**

🚆 Hanshin Uozaki

How to get there:

To reach the Hakutsuru sake brewery, take the Hanshin Electric Railway. Also called the Hanshin Main Line, this railway links Osaka and Kobe and can be picked up at Osaka Umeda station. Take the Hanshin line toward Kobe and exit your train at Uozaki station. As you exit the train station turnstiles, use the south exit which will be on your left. There is also a little pastry shop/café in the station – as you approach the south exit, it will also be on your left. Head down the stairs, make a right, and cross the bridge in front of you. After crossing the bridge, look left - there will be a staircase leading down to the

river. Take this staircase down and walk next to the river for a few minutes. You will pass beneath the Hanshin Expressway. Once under the expressway, look to your right and you will see another staircase leading back up. Use this staircase. Continue south until you reach a crossroads. At the intersection turn right and walk to the end of the street - you will pass by the Kikumasamune sake brewery. At the end of the street turn right. Walk about a block down the street then turn left. Keep an eye out for signs and the brewery will be on your right. There is a big sign out front, and a path that leads to the entrance of the brewery and sake museum.

The Brewery:

Hakutsuru is one of the world's largest sake producers and you will certainly encounter this brand back home. Pay attention:

KOBE

Hakutsuru's sake is served in Japanese restaurants all over the world and enjoys wide distribution in supermarkets and bodegas. A visit to Hakutsuru will guarantee a lifetime of satisfaction, ensuring first-hand knowledge of this pervasive global brand. Hakutsuru's company motto is "To friendship for life," and the friendly atmosphere at this sake brewery accurately reflects this sentiment.

The establishment includes a museum and sake shop in one large facility. The museum and sake production facility are on the same plot of land, but look for the old building which is the museum, and you can't miss it. Inside are pamphlets in English that explain about the sake and the brewing process at Hakutsuru. As you follow the self-guided tour around the brewery you will see many examples of how the traditional brewing process takes place, with life-sized mannequins acting out the specific duties required for brewing sake. Along the way you will also see video screens featuring individual explanations on the step-by-step brewing process. The tour will progress to the second floor where they explain how moto is made and how rice is spread out as they prepare to make koji. You will make your way through the steaming room and eventually back downstairs to where the original sake presses are held. The tour ends with a free tasting of a few different varieties of sake available for that day, usually consisting of two types of sake, one umeshu, one type of citrus wine, and generally one specialty type of sake such as nigori or lightly effervescent sake. After finishing the tasting you will end up back to the front of the store where you can stock up on sake, delicious treats, and souvenirs to bring back home.

History:

The Kano family established the Hakutsuru sake brewery in 1743. The brewery has been in continuous ownership by the Kano family since opening, with the most senior male member now being Kenji Kano. The Kano family has a rich history – Kenji's grandfather originated the sport of judo. Today the toji is Miyata Hiroshi.

KOBE

Hakutsuru continues today as one of Japan's largest producers and exporters of sake. They have always been on the cutting edge, coupling new technology with traditional methods to produce the finest sake possible at the volumes desired. Hakutsuru was one of the first breweries during the early 1900's to use electricity to help with the washing of rice and powering of small machinery to help with the brewing process. Hakutsuru has always employed at least three toji to direct their brewing activities.

Hakutsuru has believed in the quality of their product since the beginning and have always used the same rice from the same grower in the Rokko mountains. Each year, Hakutsuru makes a special batch of sake to be bottled in traditional containers and uses these bottles during sake contests. They have not always received top prizes but have consistently done very well. Among connoisseurs, consistency in achieving medals in competition is perhaps more valuable than a one-time top medal.

Final Thoughts:

This is one of the most conventionally tourist friendly breweries in Nada. The brewery is set up so that travelers from any country can visit a traditional sake brewery and learn about sake production at their own pace. For the overall experience at the brewery, generous tasting, and value of visiting one of the world's most pervasive bands, I highly recommend the visit.

KOBE

Hamafukutsuru Sake Brewery

4-4-6, Uozaki Minami - Machi, Higashi Nada - Ku, Kobe Japan
http://www.hamafukutsuru.co.jp/index.html
Shop +078-411-0492
Shop Tuesday - Sunday 10:00AM - 5:00PM closed Monday,
and any Monday following a holiday
Hanshin Uozaki

How to get there:

The easiest route to the Hamafukutsuru sake brewery is via
the Hanshin Electric Railway line. Start by exiting the train at
Uozaki station. As you exit the train station turnstiles, take a
left and go down the stairs. Proceed left along the road for
roughly two minutes. Once you reach the end of the street
turn right. Follow this street until you reach the Hanshin expressway. When you get to this point you will see a bridge to
take over the road.

KOBE

Cross the bridge, then make a left and continue south. About a block down you will see a sign for the Hamafukutsuru brewery. Ignore this sign and continue straight. You will continue about another block and then turn right. The brewery will then be on your right. Keep an eye out for the Hamafukutsuru signs. Note: there are maps of the area posted everywhere with breweries highlighted and it will generally be pretty difficult for you to get lost here, so keep an eye out.

The Brewery:

The facilities at Hamafukutsuru are quite large as they are part of the actual production sake brewery. When you walk in the front entrance you will be in the main shop. Here you can ask for a tour of the facilities. Tours normally require a reservation but if you are here before 12PM on a weekday you will have a good chance of being led on a private tour. The tour continues

KOBE

with a short walk through the upper floor where you can see the production of sake as it is made in the brewery.

After the tour you will be brought back to the main show room where you can taste every variety of sake produced at Hamafukutsuru. One of the best things about this brewery is the number and variety of sake they produce. They make about a dozen varieties spanning the various sake grades. Hamafukutsuru also produces about three different kinds of umeshu, two varieties of citrus fruit sake, cask-aged sake (taru sake), and four specialty types of sake including a milk-style sake which is only lightly (2%) alcoholic. I was told this amazake is perfect for children (what would the folks back home say?!) during months of celebration as it is also very sweet.

History:

The Brewery has been owned by the Koyama family since opening in 1808, with the most senior member now being Keiji Koyama. When Hamafukutsuru first opened it quickly became one of the biggest producers in Kobe. Because of this they were able to open roughly 63 plants, five of which were in Nada area with the others spread across the rest of Kansai, with most facilities being in Kobe and Osaka. However, the recent rise of many other big name brands of sake as well as hundreds of small local breweries, has caused a significant loss in market share, and Hamafukutsuru now only operate a fraction of the original capacity, something around 20 breweries. They used to brew sake year round but now focus on the traditional time-frame: November through March. Interestingly, Hamafukutsuru has never had one head toji. Hamafukutsuru feels that all employees that help with the sake production have an equal say in the proper way to produce the finest product.

Final Thoughts:

The staff at Hamafukutsuru speak some English but the more you can prepare with phrases from this book, the better experience you will have. Everyone in Kobe roots for the Hanshin Tigers and the staff here are no exception, so you

KOBE

might want to ask them how their Tigers are doing this year. This is a great brewery to visit and tour because it is one of the few left in Nada that still lets the public view production sake brewing right in the plant. I also find the tours here to be just the right length time-wise. The staff are very insightful and it is interesting to see the sake brewing process take place. It is also nice to able to taste everything they have in stock – there is plenty of variety and all of the tasting is free of charge. Good news for us cheapskates! The shop carries a huge selection of food gifts and other assorted goods. For overall friendliness and high sake educational value, Hamafukutsuru is high on my recommendation list.

KOBE

Izumi Yonosuke Shoten

1-2-7 Mikage Tsukamachi, Higashinada Ward, Kobe City
Brewery +078-851-2722 Daily 9AM-5PM
Closed November ~ February Hanshin Ishiyagawa

KOBE

How to get there:

From Kyoto or Osaka, there's fast and easy access to the Izumi Yonosuke Shonten sake brewery in Nada via the Hanshin Electric Railway Line. Start by exiting your train at Ishiyagawa station. Take the southern exit. Walk south about a block and there will be a crosswalk that leads to a trail next to the river. You will walk down this path for about 5 minutes before reaching the Hanshin expressway road. There will be a bridge that can be taken to cross to the other side. Once on the other side of the bridge, continue south a little less than a block until you reach another bridge. Cross the second bridge, turn left at the first intersection, and travel down this street a little. The brewery will be on your left.

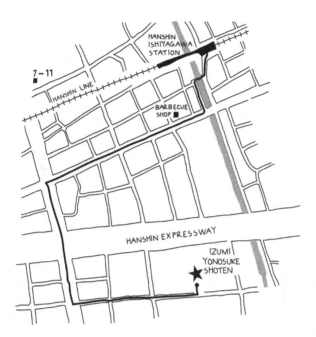

The Brewery:

The facilities at Izumi Yonosuke Shonten include a modest production sake brewery. Normally the owners do not mind taking small groups on tours if you show up on a lazy day. I was fortunate enough to catch the owner to ask him a few questions, and he told me they are working hard to upgrade their facilities and meet current demand for their sake.

History:

The brewery was built in 1882 and has been continuously owned by the Yonosuke family since opening, with its most senior member now being Izumi Yonosuke. Izumi Yonosuke Shonten is among a handful of brewers in the Kobe area to produce all of their sake by hand using traditional methods. They have recently been severely under production for the volume they've been trying to sell, and have decided to build a bigger facility and to start using machines in their production process. When I spoke with the owner he assured me that most of the brewing process will remain the same. Currently two people

KOBE

run the brewery: Yonosuke Sr. and his toji, Nakara Ikyo. The pair have been working together for over 30 years providing Kobe with quality handmade sake. The brewery doesn't usually hire more than a dozen people during the brewing season and has but a few people on staff during the rest of the year. It is a very laid back brewery with a small family feel.

Final Thoughts:

The quality of sake being made at Izumi Yonosuke Shonten is noticeable indeed. The brewery itself is quiet and out of the way. Unless you call ahead, don't expect to find someone to talk to you immediately upon arrival. You'll likely have to fish someone out of the brewery to ask a few questions and perhaps offer to buy a bottle or request a tour. Breweries like Izumi Yonosuke Shonten are the reason I wrote this book – they're wonderful and off the beaten track. There aren't any glossy brochures leading you here and no dedicated marketing staff to show you around, but if you can visit Izumi Yonosuke Shonten and share a glass of delicious sake with the guys that make it, you'll be glad you did.

KOBE

In Kobe, a friend is
never far away.

KOBE

Kikumasamune Sake Museum

1-9-1, Uozaki - Nishimachi, Higashinada - Ku, Kobe, 658-0026
Japan
http://www.kikumasamune.com/index.html
📱 Shop +078-854-1029 📠 Fax +078-854-1028
🕐 Shop daily 9:30AM-4:30PM
Last admittance into museum at 4:00PM 🚆 Hanshin Uozaki

How to get there:

The easiest route to access Kikumasamune is from the Hanshin
line. Start by exiting at Uozaki station. Take the south exit (left as
you exit the gates from the station) and head down the stairs.
Once you are down the stairs you will see a convenience store
called "Daily Yamazaki." Proceed right and cross the bridge in
front of you. After crossing the bridge, head south (to your left).
Keep an eye out for a staircase leading down to the river.

KOBE

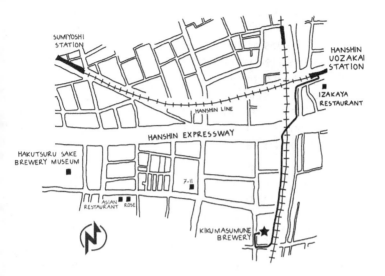

Go down these stairs. You will walk next to the river for a few minutes and pass beneath the Hanshin expressway. After you've passed beneath the expressway, look to your right and you will see another staircase leading back up. Once up, continue south until you reach a crossroad. You will see the brewery and a massive Kikumasamune tower on your right. When you reach the intersection, turn right and the entrance to the brewery will be almost immediately on your right.

The Brewery:

The facilities include a museum and sake shop. The museum is directly in front of the newer facility where they brew the actual Kikumasamune sake. The museum, curated by the affable and erudite Mr. Takaharu Asai is a bona fide historical site complete with replicas of the old brewery gear showing the facility as well as tools and machinery of old. English videos and pamphlets are available upon request. There are two videos; one about Kikumasamune's process of brewing sake through the traditional technique of kimoto-zukuri and the other on taru sake (cask sake). On the second floor you can view a collection of choko and sakazuki, with some dating back to the Edo period. The museum provides signs written in both English and Japanese that explain the brewing process. The shop offers up roughly 8 varieties of Kikumasamune's famous karakuchi (dry) sake as well as a few varieties of its delicious taru sake. All types of sake are available for tasting but you will need to request which ones you would like. The varieties they have available for tasting will be marked with a label on the bottle in the show room. The shop also features tempting hand crafted goods available for purchase.

History:

The Kikumasamune brewery was built in 1659 in the Nada district of Kobe has been owned by the Kano family since opening with the most senior member now being Mr. Taketo Kano. The unique kimoto brewing process, coupled with natural spring water from the Rokko mountains, results in a brew for which only Kikumasamune is known.

Kikumasamune is famous for two types of sake. First is their karakuchi sake. They make this through the traditional method of kimoto-zukuri. This is a method that promotes yeast growth through the use of lactic acids produced by naturally occurring bacteria. Today, many breweries will forgo growing their own lactic acid producing bacterium and simply add the lactic acid to the moto during the early stages of the brewing process. In the Edo period, all breweries used kimoto (or a similar method known as yamahai) for making sake, since they knew nothing of yeast or bacteria. The just knew that endless stirring and singing produced the desired results. Kikumasamune still believes employing naturally occurring bacteria for lactic acid is a critical step in the production of superior dry sake. During the brewing process, a step known as moto-fumi takes place in which the brewers mash the rice and koji with their feet, a practice very similar to that of crushing wine grapes. Alas, today they no longer employ traditional methods but use special rubber boots instead... you may have to visit Mr. Asai to understand what I'm talking about. You'll be glad you did.

KOBE

The other sake for which Kikumasamune is famous is their bottled version of taru sake. Taru sake is left in a cask to age and acquire its more smoky wood taste. Now you can taste this without acquiring a gigantic $500 keg of sake (as you and your friends might do if you were getting married, christening a new building, etc.).

Final Thoughts:

The staff at Kikumasamune are extremely generous, and if you use very simple English words and phrases you will get by with no problem. This is one of the easier breweries to visit, so if you're in Kobe with time to visit only one or two breweries, I would make visiting Kikumasamune a priority. The pamphlets and videos are very informative and explain how much time and energy is spent to make the kimoto sake they brew. If you enjoy dry, flavorful sake, that can be easily enjoyed when warmed or paired with all kinds of cuisine, do be sure to visit this facility to view and taste what they have to offer.

You may enjoy a junmai kimoto such as Kikumasamune produces when paired with grilled meats, teppan-style dining, and with burgers or Mexican food. These dry kimoto sake are especially delicious when paired with heartier fare, and you should try as many as you can while visiting Japan.

So much sake, so little time. But you are in Japan so make time to taste the local beer as well!

Kobe Shushinkan

1-8-17 MIKAGETSUKA, HIGASHINADA, KOBE, HYOGO 658-0044 JAPAN

📱 Shop Tel:+81-78-841-1121 📠 Fax:+81-78-841-0002
📱 Restaurant Tel:+81-78-841-2612 📠 Fax:+81-78-811-4141
🕐 Sake shop open daily 10am to 6pm. Restaurant 11am to 2:30pm, 5pm to 10pm. Both are open 7 days a week.
🚊 Hanshin Ishiyagawa

How to get there:

Reach the Kobe Shushinkan sake brewery by taking the Hanshin Electric Railway. Exit your train at Ishiyagawa station and head south. After walking about a block there will be a crosswalk that leads to a path down by the river. Take this path. You will follow the path for about 5 minutes before reaching the Hanshin expressway road. There will be a bridge in front of you - cross the bridge. Once you're on the other side of the

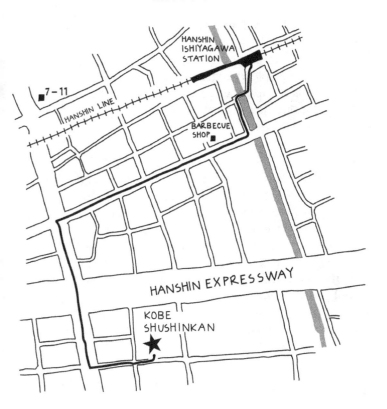

river, continue south and turn right at the first road you see. Then travel approximately two blocks down this street and the Kobe Sushinkan sake brewery will be on your right. Look for the sign!

The Brewery:

The Kobe Shushinkan sake brewery has two areas that are accessible to the general public without a reservation: a sake shop and restaurant. Production facility tours are available but do require a reservation. The brewery is open all year and is only closed the first few days of January. There is no charge to tour the brewery and you can also taste all the sake they have free of charge.

KOBE

Kobe Sushinkan does a great job on basic sake education, showing how the rice grain is milled to obtain the sought-after taste. A few pamphlets covering the sake brewing process and a video are available in English. Tours of the production facilities are available upon request but you must make a reservation at least one day in advance. Production facility tours are only available on weekdays.

History:

The Kobe Sushinkan sake brewery was established in 1751 by the Takenosuke family. The brewery has been in continuous ownership with the senior member of the family currently being Yasufuku Takenosuke. When the brewery first opened it was run by one head brewer who employed about 14 other local men to help with the brewing process. Today there are 6 brew masters, each toji being of a similar rank and each contributing his knowledge and experience. Interestingly, Kobe Shushinkan is known as one of the only breweries left in Japan that still uses the wood press method to obtain the final product after fermentation. The brewery believes that this tried and true method of pressing the moto brings a distinct taste and quality to the sake that many other brewers have long abandoned.

Final Thoughts:

Expect to be treated very kindly when you visit the Kobe Sushinkan sake brewery. When I lead tours to this brewery I rely on an interpreter or a friend fluent in Japanese to help, although the brewery does employ a few English and French speakers. If you're visiting the facilities here without my assistance, make a reservation in advance and also try to have a Japanese speaker with you to maximize your enjoyment of everything they have to offer.

The facilities here are immaculate and the presentation of the sake for tasting is particularly unique and informative. If you have the assistance of a guide or a native speaker, your experience will be truly unforgettable.

KOBE

When presented with a selection of sake,
a true master always chooses both.

KOBE

Sakuramasamune Sakuraen

5-10-1 Uozakiminami-machi, Higashinada-ku, Kobe, JAPAN
http://www.sakuramasamune.co.jp/english.html
📱 Shop +81-78-411-2101   📠 Fax +81-78-411-2102
🕐 Shop daily 10AM-10PM   🚆 Hanshin Uozaki

How to get there:

Sakuramasamune Sakuren is easily reached via the Hanshin Electric Railway line, running between Osaka and Kobe. Hop off your train at Uozaki station and take the south exit. As you exit the station's turnstiles, the south exit will be to your left. Take the stairs down, proceed right, and cross the bridge in front of you. After crossing the bridge, look to your left and you will see a staircase leading down to the river. Take this staircase. You will walk next to the river for a few minuets and pass beneath the Hanshin expressway. When you have passed beneath the expressway, look to your right and you will see another staircase leading back up. Walk up the stairs. Once up, continue south until you reach a crossroad. At the intersection, proceed left across the river and travel roughly two blocks. Then make another left. Go down the road a little and the brewery will be on your right.

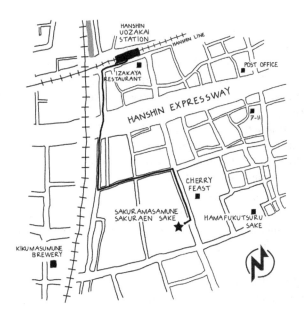

The Brewery:

The facilities at Sakuramasamune Sakuren include a small museum and sake shop as well as a cafe and fine dining restaurant. The museum is small but comprehensive, and takes up the second floor as you first walk into the facility. The shop provides a selection of sake for tasting which is available free of charge. The cafe located inside is quaint and you can purchase snacks, ice cream, and sandwiches here. You can also go upstairs and make reservations at the very nice restaurant they have on site. For a personal tour of the production facilities, call ahead to make a reservation.

History:

Sakuramasamune is an old, storied brewer of sake in Nada. They claim to have invented both the idea of milled rice (and hence premium ginjo sake), as well as to have discovered miyamizu, the water that lends its qualities to so many of the fine brewers of sake in Nada. The Yamamura family started brewing sake in 1625 and the brewery in Nada has been in the

KOBE

family since they first opened their doors in 1717. Sakurama-samune was one of the first breweries established in Nada, and many attribute their current success to this longevity.

You will notice other breweries in Japan that use "masamune" as the second part of their name. The kanji characters for masamune are similar to the word "seishu" – the legal word for nihonshu or sake. Thus, masamune became a synonym for Sakuramasamune's sake, and for sake itself. Though Sakuramasamune is rumored to be the first to use masamune, and tried to register this as a trademark, the registration was denied because the word "masamune" had fallen into regular use as a word for sake.

The brewery is located across the street from the shop and small museum. Tours are available but reservations must be made in advance.

Final Thoughts:

Visiting Sakuramasamune Sakuren in Nada can be considered something of a pilgrimage for sake fans. It has one of the fanciest sake shops in Nada, as well as a fine dining restaurant. By all means stop by Sakuramasamune on your visit to Nada. However, do not show up for a tour without a reservation – you'll find the staff scrambling to accommodate your request, and calling headquarters in Tokyo to ask what they should do with you!

KOBE

*You know you're close
when you see signs
like this...*

KOBE

Sawanotsuru Sake Museum

1-29-1, Oishi-minami-machi, Nada - Ku, Kobe, Hyogo 657-0864
Japan
http://www.sawanotsuru.net/
📱 Shop +078-882-7788 📠 Fax +078-882-6777
🕐 Shop daily 10:00AM-4:00PM closed Wednesday, Holidays,
Bon-festivals, mid August, New Years 🚃 Hanshin Oishi

How to get there:

The easiest way to access the Sawanotsuru Sake Museum is
via the Hanshin Main Line. You will start by exiting your train
at Oishi station. Take the south exit. Proceed straight until you
reach the Hanshin expressway. On your right, there will be an
underground passage that leads to the other side of the road.
Once on the other side continue south for another 5 minutes.
You will eventually see a map with directions to all the sake
breweries at a fork in the road. Take the right part of the fork
and continue straight, and the brewery will appear immediately on your right.

KOBE

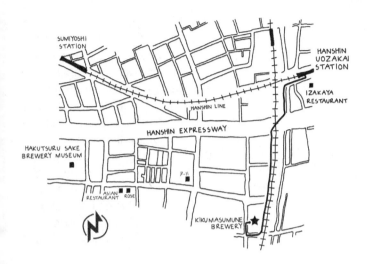

The Brewery:

The facilities include a museum and separate sake shop. This was the place of the original brewery that was destroyed during the great Hanshin earthquake of 1995, and it was rebuilt to showcase the original facility as well as the tools used in traditional sake making. The museum is quite large and features two floors worth of history for you to enjoy. Every aspect of the brewing process is covered in this museum from the polishing of rice and the pressing of sake, to the shipping across all of Japan. From the second floor you can access a staircase that will take you behind the museum to the sake shop.

Sawanotsuru produces about a dozen varieties of sake with a few specialty brews such as umeshu and citrus sake. Generally there is only one type of sake available for tasting each day, but if requested it's possible to try a few more. The shop sells a wide array of food and gifts.

KOBE

History:

The brewery was established in 1717, right here in the Nada district of Kobe – as you know, one of the most important areas for sake brewing in Japan. The brewery has been owned by the Nishimura family since opening, with the most senior member now being Takaharu Nishimura. Sawanotsuru has long been one of the few remaining original sake breweries in the Nada district that has continued to use traditional methods and tools to produce sake. After the original plant was rebuilt into a museum, Sawanotsuru earned recognition as a national heritage site of Japan. The new factory was subsequently built right behind the original plant. Sawanotusru now uses modern technology for its production of sake but still keeps a few traditional styles including kimoto-zukuri. The new production facilities have won the gold medal at the national sake awards 3 times in a row for Daiginjo sake.

Much of Sawanotsuru's recent success is attributed to their current toji, Dekuji Kikuji. Sawanotsuru has enjoyed rapid growth in premium sake sales through global exports. It was also one of the first breweries to coin the terms used for temperature differentiation when consuming sake during different seasons.

Final Thoughts:

Sawanotsuru is recognized as one of the founding breweries in Nada and receives much recognition locally and worldwide. If you want to enjoy a very traditional brewery that has been replicated exactly as it once was, and at your own pace without the crowds, visiting Sawanotsuru should be a priority. As one of the Nada's founding breweries, it also has its own unique charm to it that the larger, more highly polished global sake producers have somehow lost.

KOBE

The Four Seasons of the Japanese Cuisine

Japan stretches North-East to South-West, from the snow-covered Hokkaido mountains to the tropical beaches of Okinawa and its various islands. The weather extremes of its northern and southern tips aside, most of Japan enjoys a temperate climate, marked by distinct seasonal variation.

The change of seasons is deeply important to the Japanese psyche. The beauty of each season is celebrated in art and literature, and serves as a particular point of national pride. To a foreigner, the notion of uniquely Japanese seasons could seem naïve and inward-looking, as if the Japanese refuse to acknowledge the presence of four seasons elsewhere in the world. However, behind this infatuation with seasons is the Japanese system of beliefs.

Shinto, the indigenous religion of Japan, considers nature to be a manifestation of the divine. Shinto gods and goddesses, *kami*, are sacred spirits that take the form of natural phenomena; wind, rain, ocean, mountains, sun. Humans reunite with nature

after their death, themselves becoming kami. Thus, the Japanese spirituality centers upon living in harmony with nature, and views the change of seasons as the time to renew and transform, affirming people's connection with the divine nature.

Buddhism, the second most dominant religion in Japan, also plays a part. The changing of the seasons is the perfect symbol of the Buddhist mujō, the transience of all things in life.

Each season brings a round of religious rites, festivals, and rituals designed to show appreciation for nature and its gifts. Whether they are Shintoist, Buddhist, or a mix of both, people join in with gusto in all of the festivities. Food, of course, is an inextricable part of every celebration – and often the most important!

Spring

In spring, people gather for cherry blossom viewing parties, called hanami. Cheerful families and raucous groups of work colleagues spread out picnic blankets under the blooming sakura trees to enjoy the ephemeral beauty of the blossoms. Within hours of reaching full bloom, the flowers begin to shed their petals onto the ground. To the Japanese, this short-lived glory is the perfect metaphor for the Buddhist teachings of the brevity of human life.

The original, lesser known reason for celebrating sakura blossoming is the Shinto belief that sakura is the earthly manifestation of the god of rice fields. The god would go into the mountains after the fall harvest and return in spring when the sakura bloomed. The farmers would (and still do in some areas) entertain the god by feasting and dancing once the flowers reached full bloom. After the petals have all fallen onto the ground, it was time to plant the rice.

The Japanese take preparations for hanami very seriously. From early March, Japanese newspapers begin tracking the cherry blossom front – the timing of sakura blossoming that begins in the south of Kyushu. As the cherry blossom front (sakura zensen) moves towards them, the housewives and chefs begin preparations for hanami bento, boxed meals consumed at hanami parties.

Hanami bento are packed with seasonal ingredients, some of them selected to fit the red and pink sakura theme. New season bamboo shoots, so fresh they can be eaten raw, canola blossoms (na no hana), carrots cut into the shape of flowers, prawns, and salmon make a frequent appearance. Chirashi-zushi – raw fish, grated egg omelet and vegetables scattered over vinegared rice – is a popular hanami bento choice. Pink-colored rice dumplings (dango) and even rice balls stuffed with salted cherry blossoms (sakura onigiri) are also seasonal favorites.

Hanami bento can be purchased practically anywhere during the cherry blossom season. Bento street stalls and convenience stores all sell them, but the most reliable place to source a hanami bento would be a department store. Japanese department stores dedicate basement levels (depachika) to gourmet food and drink, and the choice of delicacies for sale is usually overwhelming.

Of course, no hanami is complete without sake. Drinking sake – as opposed to beer or wine – is a quintessential hanami tradition. Giant 1.8 liter sake bottles, issho-bin, are popular with rowdy gatherings, but you can pick up a more manageable quantity of sake in the department store food hall, right after selecting your hanami bento.

Summer

The mighty ume

June marks the beginning of the rainy season in Japan. Throughout most of the country, it lasts until the middle of July, although the Okinawa islands experience the rainy season a month earlier. Hokkaido hardly feels its effects.

The rainy season is called **tsuyu**, which literally means "plum rain" or "ume rain". Ume is commonly known as Japanese apricot. It is actually a distinct fruit tree species originating from China, although closely related to both apricot and plum. June is the time of the year when ume fruit ripens and the Japanese begin making pickled plums (*umeboshi)* and plum wine (*umeshu*).

The ume tree has long played an important part in Japanese culture and cuisine. Plum blossoms have a claim to fame as the original object of adoration at flower viewing parties, until cherry blossoms took over during the Heian period (AD 794-1185).

Ume fruit was also prized in zen culture and samurai society. Zen monks took green tea with *umeboshi* (salt-pickled *plums*) to purge evil thoughts and prepare for ascetic training. Medieval doctors attributed all sorts of healing qualities to ume, and feudal lords planted ume trees in preparation for wars.

The modern-day Japanese folk enjoy ume just as much. A pickled ume or two is a frequent guest in bento lunches, and rice balls (*onigiri*) with umeboshi is a popular snack. Umeboshi onigiri can be found in any convenience store. Grilled chicken is often topped with umeboshi sauce.

Another popular incarnation of ume is the sweet ume

liquor *umeshu* (it often goes by the moniker "plum wine"). Umeshu is made by steeping ume fruit in shochu or sake for about a year. It has a distinct, rather enjoyable flavor, and is often served on the rocks. Addictive stuff, and fast becoming popular overseas.

The festival season

Summer is the season of festivals. Three events rule supreme: Tanabata, Obon and the fireworks festival.

Tanabata is the star festival that usually takes place on the 7th of July. It originates from a Chinese legend of two stars, Vega and Atair, who are torn apart by the gods and only allowed to reunite once a year. People write wishes on long, colorful ribbons of paper and hang them from specially erected bamboo poles in the hopes that their wishes come true.

Obon is the Buddhist festival celebrating ancestral spirits. Across Japan, from August 13th to 16th, people prepare their homes for the visit of their ancestors. They make offerings of food at the Buddhist altar, hang a lantern in front of the house to guide the spirits home, and at night go out and join crowds at bon-odori, the Obon festival dancing. At the end of Obon, the paper lanterns that welcomed the spirits are illuminated and set floating down rivers to symbolize the ancestral spirits' return to the world of the dead.

Many restaurants close for the Obon period, especially those serving high-class traditional cuisine.

The one celebration that most Japanese look forward to the most is **hanabi,** the fireworks festival. Just like sakura blossoms, the flowers blooming in the sky are admired for their brief beauty – and the opportunity to party. The competition for spots to watch fireworks is perhaps even more intense than for spots under sakura trees. The atmosphere is indeed festive. Young women wear colorful summer kimono (*yukata)*, food stalls line the streets, and sake flows freely.

For a traveler, festivals give the best chance to try Japanese street food. The ever-popular choices are takoyaki (grilled balls of dough with cabbage and octopus inside, served with mayonnaise, special takoyaki sauce, and dried bonito flakes), yakitori (small skewers of chicken grilled over charcoal), taiyaki (fish-shaped pancake shells with sweet filling, such as red bean paste or custard), yakisoba (fried noodles with vegetables and meat), and the ultimate summer delicacy, whole roasted ayu (sweetfish).

Fall (autumn)

Fall in Japan is defined by the cornucopia of foliage colors (kōyō). The kōyō front (kōyō zensen) moves in the direction opposite to the cherry blossom front. It starts in September in the mountains of Hokkaido and ends in southern Kyushu by early December. In Tokyo and Kyoto, maple and gingko trees turn into every shade of yellow, orange, and red by the middle of November.

The Japanese pursue the sport of kōyō with the same vigor they apply to viewing sakura and fireworks, traveling across prefectures in search of the very best multi-colored vistas.

Perhaps the less obvious object of adoration is the September moon. Moon viewing (**otsukimi)** is both the aesthetic pursuit and the tradition steeped in Shinto belief in the spirits of nature. September moon viewing is when the Japanese give thanks for the fall harvest. They make offerings of seasonal produce – taro potatoes, persimmons, chestnuts, and pumpkins - at family altars and set up dinner tables outside to sup under moonlight. Moon harvest festivals are also celebrated in Shinto shrines.

These celebrations are echoed in restaurants serving traditional *kaiseki* cuisine. The chefs work to evoke the scenes and smells of the season. They work fall leaves into the presentation of dishes, serve rice cooked with chestnuts and matsutake mushrooms, and grill fish over charcoal until it smokes, evoking the smell of burning leaves. Visiting a kaiseki restaurant in fall is a special treat indeed.

The scenes of temples and shrines drowning in the explosion of colors, the seasonal delicacies and most importantly, the near-perfect weather, make fall one of the best times to visit Japan.

Winter

As far as seasonal events go, there is one to rule them all – the New Year, or **shōgatsu**. Throughout December, restaurants and pubs are booked out for bōnenkai, the rowdy year-end parties. Groups of friends and colleagues drink and make lots of noise with the idea to forget the bad times of the past year. The New Year, however, is a family celebration, and the closest one can get to a party is to join the crowds visiting temples and shrines overnight.

On New Year's eve (ōmisoka), families gather to eat soba in the hope of life as long as the thin buckwheat noodles. The soba must be finished before the bells at a nearby Buddhist temple ring out the old year with 108 strikes – lest bad luck falls upon the eater!

The first day of the year is the holiest in Japan, when families make the first visit to the shrine to pray for the New Year's happiness. They eat specially prepared, traditional foods that symbolise all the things they hope to receive in the coming hear – **osechi ryōri**.

Osechi ryori is big business in Japan. In the past, every family spent days, or even weeks, preparing the special foods they ate over the first three days of the New Year (no cooking was allowed on those holy days). The foods were made to last a while, and kept in compartmentalized stacked boxes. Each morsel meant something – fish roe a wish for many children, sardines a symbol for abundant harvest (sardines used to be a fertilizer), shrimp a desire to live until old age. These days, time-poor people are more likely to buy osechi. Prices start from just under $100 for a basic supermarket version to *thousands* of dollars for osechi ryori ordered from a famous restaurant or a fancy department store.

Osechi isn't something you will see on a menu in a restaurant, but the department stores' splendid display of deluxe osechi in beautiful lacquer boxes is worth checking out. Pick any department store catalogue and the pages will be filled with eye-wateringly expensive osechi choices. The Shinto symbolism of each ingredient is balanced with Japanese presentation aesthetics, resulting in food that is almost too pretty to eat. If you are game to try it, osechi must be reserved by the 20th of December.

On the other side of the spectrum is decidedly un-Japanese, but nevertheless very popular, Christmas cake tradition. In department stores and patisseries, Christmas cake order counters start operating from as early as October. Christians make up a very small minority in Japan, but the Japanese have almost beaten out the Western world in Christmas commercialization stakes. The Christmas cake tradition, though, is not half as bad – Japanese confectioners have skills to rival those of their French counterparts, and purchasing an exquisitely detailed Christmas cake to share with family or friends does have an element of true Christmas spirit to it.

Seasonal Glossary	
Seasonal food	Shun no mono
Just in season	Chyōdo shun
I would like to eat seasonal food.	Watashi wa shun no mono o tabetai.
Spring	**Haru**
"Lazy sushi" – seafood and vegetable scattered over rice	Chirashi-zushi
Canola blossoms	Na-no-hana
Clear soup with hard clams and seasonal vegetables	Hamaguri no osuimono
Bamboo shoots	Take (tah-keh), take no ko
Sea bream roe, the deluxe spring ingredient typically only found in ryōtei, high-class restaurants	Tai no tamago
Rice ball stuffed with salted cherry blossom petals	Sakura onigiri
Summer	**Natsu**
GrilLed, salted sweetfish	Ayu no shio-yaki
Eel grilled with sweet soy sauce	Unagi no kaba-yaki
Chilled tofu with toppings, such as katsuobushi (dried skipjack tuna flakes), green onion, and soy	Hiya-yakko
Cold soba noodles topped with shredded nori seaweed, served with a dipping sauce of soy, shredded shallots, and wasabi. Great on a hot day!	Zaru-soba
Chilled, thin wheat noodles served with grated ginger, sliced scallion, and other toppings	Sōmen

Shaved ice with various sweet toppings, a popular summer dessert	Kakigōri
Fall	**Aki**
Baked sweet potato (sold from numerous street stalls)	Yaki-imo
Chestnuts	Kuri, maron
Grilled eggplant	Yaki-nasu
Grilled Pacific saury	Sanma no shio-yaki
Pine mushrooms	Matsutake
Rice cooked with chestnuts	Kuri gohan
Rice cooked with pine mushrooms	Matutake gohan
Pumpkin	Kabocha
Winter	**Fuyu**
Crab (king crab is at the seasonal best)	Kani
King crab, a Hokkaido delicacy at its seasonal best	Taraba-gani
Crab hotpot	Kani nabe
Sumo stew, a hearty stew of meats and vegetables eaten by sumo wrestlers to gain weight. It is pretty healthy!	Chanko-nabe
Hotpot cuisine	Nabe-ryori
Blowfish (also commonly called pufferfish or globefish)	Fugu
New Year dishes	Osechi-ryōri
Christmas cake	Ku-ris-ma-su-kē-ki

Kaiseki – the Japanese Haute Cuisine

Nothing showcases the skills of Japanese chefs like kaiseki cuisine.

Kaiseki is a formal multi-course dinner that is all about simple preparation of fresh, local, and seasonal ingredients. Kaiseki began as the Imperial court cuisine during the Heian period (9th century). It was significantly refined in Kyoto during the 15th-16th centuries as the food accompanying the highly formal tea ceremony. Kyoto is still leading the way, as Japanese and international food critics consider Kyoto kaiseki restaurants (ryōtei) the best of their kind.

Every aspect of hospitality is carefully considered: the décor, ceramics, and visual presentation of dishes as well as, the service. The chefs aim to highlight the beauty of each ingredient and to create a harmony of colors, shapes, and textures on a plate. Such perfection doesn't come cheap, however, and the diner is likely to part with at least $100 at dinner time, often much more. There is a way to cut the cost, though, by going for lunch instead of dinner. In Japan, lunch prices can sometimes be as low as one third of the price of dinner.

The traditional Japanese dinner follows a certain flow. It begins with a small snack, followed by a hassun platter of seasonal appetizers that highlight the mood, colors, and flavors of the season. Then comes a procession of dishes showcasing different cooking methods – sashimi course, steamed course, grilled course, soup course, tempura course. The meal finishes with a bowl of rice, miso soup, and pickles. Historically, the rice was served to fill up the guests at the end of a protracted meal consisting of tiny morsels of food. These days, kaiseki portions are larger, so you might struggle to finish all the rice. However, it is polite to do so, as the Japanese frown upon left over rice and picky eaters in general. If there is no chance of you finishing your meal, ask for the rice to be packed to go. Quite often, the chefs will prepare more rice than can be eaten so that the guests can take the ryōtei rice with gourmet filling – crab, fish roe, matsutake mushrooms, abalone – back to their families as a souvenir.

KYOTO

Kitcho Arashiyama

One of the most highly respected kaiseki restaurants in the world, this restaurant adheres to the best of the tea ceremony traditions. For each guest, the restaurant decides on the décor, serving ware and the menu individually depending on who they are, the dining occasion, and their past preferences. The restaurant holds an annual rice tasting session for its staff to decide which rice will be served in the coming year

Kitcho also has a Tokyo branch.
58 Susukinobaba0cho, Saga Tenryuji, Ukyo-ku, Kyoto
Tel. 075-881-1101
11:30 AM to 3 PM, 5 PM to 9 PM
Closed Wednesdays, December 26-31, and January 3-9.
www.kitcho.com/kyoto
Prices start from over ¥30,000 for lunch.

Kikunoi Honten

Like Kitcho, Kikunoi is the proud custodian of the finest tea ceremony traditions. It also shares the honor of having been awarded three stars by Michelin Guide Japan. Aware of its international reputation, the restaurant has an English menu and welcomes foreign guests. It has a slightly more casual sister restaurant called Kikunoi Roan nearby and a similarly formal branch in Tokyo.

459 Shimokawaracho, Shimokawara-dori Yasakatorijimae Sagaru, Higashiyama-ku, Kyoto
Tel. 075-561-0015
12 PM to 2 PM, 5 PM to 8 PM
Closed late December-early January
http://kikunoi.jp/english/

Hyotei

Presiding over the Kyoto fine dining scene for over four centuries, Hyotei is the ultimate in Japanese hospitality. Located on the Nanzenji Temple grounds, it began as a tea house for pilgrims.

It also holds three Michelin stars.

35 Kusakawacho, Nanzenji, Sakyo-ku, Kyoto
Tel. 075-771-4116
11 AM – 7:30 PM
Closed late December, every 2nd and 4th Tuesday
http://hyotei.co.jp/

OSAKA

Kashiwaya

A three Michelin star establishment, this ryōtei specializes in kaiseki with a twist, and features a traditional floor seating inspired by the tea ceremony.

2-5-18 Senriyamanishi, Suita City
Tel. 06-6386-2234
11.30 AM – 1:30 PM, 5 PM – 8 PM

Closed mid-August for Obon, late December-early January, Sunday and public holidays.

Kaishoku Shimizu

Kaishoku Shimizu is headed by a young chef who is not afraid to add his own twist to the age-old cuisine. The restaurant is kappo-style (counter seating), with the chefs preparing meals in front of you. Fish in all its manifestations – skin, guts, and even the fish sperm called shirako – are served in inventive, appetizing ways. Sashimi could be offered with a prawn brain dipping sauce, and accompanying vegetables could be of the wild variety. Kaishoku Shimizu is an exciting journey for adventurous gourmands.

2-13-31 Shimanouchi, Chuo-ku, Osaka
Tel 06-6213-3140
11.30 AM – 1 PM, 5 PM – 9 PM
Closed for Obon mid-August, late December-early January, Sunday and public holidays.
Lunch is good value, starting from just over ¥5000.

The staff speak Japanese only, and confirmation of booking is required a few days ahead since the restaurant will be purchasing ingredients for the meal option you pre-select. Best booked through your hotel concierge!

TOKYO

Kyoto's Kikunoi, Hyotei and Kitcho all have outposts in Tokyo. However, Tokyo offers its own unique flavor of the venerable kaiseki. This is a big, fast city that embraces everything cutting-edge. The following places have a global following:

Ryugin

The owner-chef Seiji Yamamoto is hailed as the Japan's top molecular gastronomist. Ryugin started out as a modern cuisine restaurant, but Yamamoto has had a change of heart in recent years and now focuses on kaiseki – with a molecular twist.

7-17-24 Roppongi, Minato-ku, Tokyo
Tel. 03-3423-8006
18 PM – 1 AM, L.O.10:30 PM
Closed for Obon mid-August, late December-early January, Sunday and public holidays. If they are unable to confirm your reservation the day before, you will be charged a ¥20,000 penalty.

Esaki

Esaki offers a contemporary version of Japanese kaiseki cuisine, focusing on organic ingredients and ethically harvested fish.

Hills Aoyama B1F
3-39-9 Jingumae, Shibuya-ku, Tokyo
Tel. 03-3408-5056
Lunch Thu.-Sat. 12 PM – 2 PM, Dinner 6 PM – 11 PM
Closed for Golden week, mid-August, late December-early January, Sunday and public holidays.
http://www.aoyamaesaki.net/

Nabura

This restaurant, with a stellar word-of-mouth reputation, has remained an insiders-only haunt by staying out of the Michelin Guide and Time Out Tokyo. Well, the secret is out! Nabura specializes in high-end, rare, and seasonal seafood served in the kaiseki format.

Roppongi Shimada Building B1
4-8-7 Roppongi, Minato-ku, Tokyo
Tel. 03 5411 3333
6 PM – 12 AM
Closed Sunday
Not just at a restaurant...

Serving kaiseki cuisine is not just the province of ryōtei restaurants. What many tourists don't know is that by staying at a traditional Japanese inn, or ryokan, you can dine on kaiseki in your room. On average, a stay in a ryokan costs a little over $150 per person per night, but that rate includes a traditional Japanese dinner served in your room (sometimes in the main restaurant) and a Japanese-style breakfast. Some of the most renowned gourmet ryokans are, of course, in Kyoto, for example Tawaraya or Hoshinoya. But the great thing about Japan is that the quality of food is not exclusive to cultural and metropolitan centres. An off-the-beaten path traveler can expect to find food that surprises and delights in every little town.

And the rest...
Kaiseki will test your wallet, but Japanese cuisine, overall, is much more democratic than that. The number of restaurants is dizzying. Tokyo alone has around 100,000 of them! To survive in such numbers, restaurants keep prices quite affordable. In fact, it is reasonable to expect to eat a quality lunch for around $8 in Tokyo.

Yakitori

Yakitori restaurants are the ultimate in Japanese informal entertainment. Technically, yakitori cuisine means chicken skewered and grilled over charcoal, but other meats and vegetables get the grilling, too. The proper term for non-poultry grilled

items is "kushiyaki", but both "yakitori" and "kushiyaki", are used interchangeably. "Yakitori" is the most common term. Yakitori restaurants do come in a deluxe version, too. Most famous is Michelin-starred Birdland in Ginza. Dare we say, it does not do justice to the unabashed fun of a typical smoke-filled, hole-in-the-wall establishment.

The perfect yakitori-eating environment is a tiny counter restaurant, where customers can interact with the chef and watch him cook tiny skewers over the binchotan-fired robata grill. Yakitori is also a menu mainstay of izakaya (Japanese pub) restaurants, as salty, savory morsels are the perfect company for sake, shochu, and beer.

When you order, the staff will ask whether you would like tare (sweet sauce made with soy, sake, and mirin) or plain salt on your meat. Salt allows smokiness to come through, while dark, sticky tare is especially delicious on liver or meatballs.

The more authentic the restaurant, the less likely English will be spoken. Yakitori cuisine is worth conquering, so carry a handy list of key dishes so that you can simply say what you would like. Each skewer costs $1 - $2.

- momo, chicken thigh
- negima, chicken intermixed with spring onion
- tsukune, chicken meatballs brushed with tare sauce
- torikawa, chicken skin grilled until crispy
- tebasaki, chicken wing
- hāto/hatsu or kokoro, chicken heart
- rebā, liver
- toriniku, white chicken meat
- yaki onigiri, onigiri rice ball brushed with tare and grilled
- ochazuke, a simple, but infinitely satisfying soup made by pouring a mixture of a meat or vegetable broth and green tea over rice. Sounds wrong, but it works!

The long strip of restaurants under the Yurakucho train tracks in Tokyo famously houses some of the best casual yakitori restaurants. Follow the smoke.

Sushi-ya

By including a smattering of Japanese cuisine, I hope you get the picture – not all food in Japan is raw fish. But ... Sushi-ya is the name for restaurants serving sushi. The important principle of selecting a sushi restaurant is that the more traditional the place appears, the more expensive it is likely to be. Noren curtains hanging over the door and liberal use of pale wood inside are tell-tale signs of the class of the establishment. The place has no menu? Carry a lot of cash. Of course, the austere, intimidating ambience of refined sushi-ya is not the only way to enjoy the fresh, abundant seafood in Japan. Take an early tour of Tsukiji fish markets in Tokyo and stop at one of many sushi-ya serving just-arrived seafood near the market exit. To quickly locate a mid-range sushi-ya in a Japanese city, head to any department store. The top level is usually the restaurant floor, and there will always be a sushi-ya in the lineup. During lunch, most restaurants will offer specially priced lunch sets, and it is reasonable to expect to dine on fresh, deftly prepared seafood for under $20.

Where you sit in a sushi-ya determines the way you order. Choosing a seat at the counter, and watching a sushi chef concentrate on his craft, is an essential experience for any traveler to Japan. Ask for omakase – chef's choice – and have a succession of weird and wonderful morsels appear in front of you. Expect to see a lot more invertebrates than in your home country. Japanese sushi chefs serve all sorts of clams, squids, and other molluscs to their hungry customers. For the risk-averse, calling out the names of seafood you would like to eat might be the way to go.

There is always the sushi-go-round, of course. Kaiten-zushi, or conveyor belt sushi restaurants, are ubiquitous in Japan – just as they are overseas. I like kaiten-zushi – it's a quick, fun, fresh, and budget-conscious meal that puts you in the way of locals – just the kind of travel you want to do. The principles are largely the same as anywhere in the world – you sit down, pour a tea from a little tap in front of you, and watch the plates as they roll on by. In the end, you'll be charged for the number of plates you pulled from the conveyor belt.

You might be surprised to find that the Japanese eat sushi by dipping the top part into soy rather than soaking the rice foundation. At times, no soy is even offered separately - the sushi comes out with a bit of sauce already dabbed on top of each piece. Wasabi is not mixed with soy, either. Pickled ginger (gari) is not intended to be heaped on top of sushi, but eaten sparingly between courses to refresh the palate. Sushi can be eaten by hand, as well as with chopsticks. It is okay to share with your dining companion, but never by passing food from chopsticks to chopsticks – this act evokes a common funeral ritual and is certain to elicit a rise of an eyebrow from the Japanese diners around you.

The best strategy is to accept the sushi the chef places in front of you just as it comes, and eat it with intrepid heart. At the end of the meal, instead of saying "o-kanjo" in reference to the bill, show off a bit of I-eat-like-a-local flair and exclaim "o-aiso!". O-aiso is the traditional sushi-ya term for indicating you are ready to go.

If the pressure of eating sushi in front of the Japanese chef is daunting, take the safest route and pick up the a box of sushi from depachika (underground food hall attached to department stores) or a supermarket. The selection of sushi is usually vast, inexpensive, and ultra fresh.

There are about 5000 sushi-ya in Tokyo. Some of the most renowned are Sukiyabashi Jiro (of *Jiro Dreams of Sushi* fame), Sushi Saito, and Daisan Harumi.

Sushi glossary

TYPES OF SUSHI	
Nigiri-zushi	balls of vinegared rice with a seafood topping. It is also called edomae-zushi, or Tokyo-style sushi. The most common kind, familiar to many around the world.
Norimaki	rolled sushi wrapped in nori seaweed.
Chirashi-zushi	"lazy" sushi, a bowl of vinegared rice with pieces of seafood, vegetables, and grated omelette scattered on top.
Inari-zushi	a pouch of fried tofu filled with vinegared rice
Oshi-zushi	Osaka-styled sushi, vinegared rice pressed into rectangular shapes topped with marinated or boiled fish.
INGREDIENTS	
Murasaki	sushi-ya term for soy sauce (usually sho-yu)
Gari	pickled ginger
Agari	sushi-ya term for green tea. Usually served at the end of the meal.
Tai	red seabream, considered the king of fish in Japan
Fugu	pufferfish
Hon-maguro	bluefin tuna
Akami	top loin of bluefin tuna
Ōtoro	fattiest portion of bluefin tuna belly
Buri	adult yellowtail
Hamachi	young yellowtail
Hatsu-katsuo	the first bonito of the season, a seasonal delicacy
Ibodai	Japanese butterfish

Aji	Japanese jack mackerel
Engawa	the thin muscle of the dorsal fin of spotted sole/halibut.
Kajiki	swordfish
Kohada	gizzard shad
Ankimo	monkfish liver, cooked
Saba	mackerel
Sake	salmon
Magochi	flathead
Anago	conger eel
Irugai aji	horse mackerel
Iwashi	sardine
Shiroshita	garei no kimo (flounder liver)
kuruma	ebi (Japanese tiger prawn)
Kaki	oyster
Ebi	shrimp
Torigai	giant cockle
Uni	sea urchin
Awabi	abalone
Akagai	ark shell
Tairagai	the adductor muscle of a pen shell
Kani	crab
tako no ashi	octopus legs
Uni	sea urchin roe
Ika	cuttlefish
Hamaguri	clam
Hotate	scallop
Ikura	salmon fish roe

Izakaya

The term "izakaya" has entered the urban vernacular far out-side Japan. "Japanese pub" or "Japanese tapas" are two common translations. Both are quite apt, since izakaya are where the Japanese go to drink, eat, and be merry. A big red lantern often hangs at the front. The menu consists of small dishes ordered throughout the evening to accompany the free-flowing alcohol. Izakayas are incredibly popular, and seem to be one of the few outlets where the Japanese can dispense with the formalities and have noisy, unabashed fun. You are as likely to encounter groups of besuited salarymen as you are gatherings of friends. The seating is tightly spaced, and clouds of tobacco smoke mingle with the smoke of the binchotan-fired grill.

The staff will seat you, take your drink order, and leave you to pour over the extensive, unintelligible menu. Scrolls with daily specials line the walls. The drink list will be heavy on beer, sake, and shochu but wine will also be on offer. In Tokyo and other metropolitan centers, more and more izakayas are beginning to offer English menus. Motion the waiter once you have decided on the food, and order. The food comes out quickly, and you are expected to continue ordering a few more morsels as you place a new order of drinks.

Reasonable prices of alcohol and food are some of the major attractions of izakayas. Many specialize in a particular type of food, such as yakitori or seafood. In truth, there is a bit of everything. Potato fries, sashimi, spicy chicken wings, grilled fish, fish cakes, noodles, stews, sushi, and salads are all usual fare. Order well, and a dinner at an izakaya could become the most memorable night of your trip.

Typical Izakaya Menu:

Sakana arani – simmered fish

Yakitori moriawase – a choice selection of skewered and grilled chicken. Refer to the yakitori section to learn what to order individually.

Nasu dengaki – eggplant grilled with sweet miso paste

Agedashi togu – deep-fried tofu served in a little broth with green onion, grated daikon and katsuobushi topping

Edamame – boiled and salted soybean pods, a popular beer accompaniment

Tsukemono – pickles

Oden moriawase – oden is food braised in soy and dashi-flavored stock. Moriawase, a selection, will probably include pieces of daikon radish, fish cakes, meat, and burdock roll

Chawan-mushi – savory steamed egg custard with fillings of meat and vegetables

Poteto furai – potato fried, usually deftly done in Japan

Ebi furai – deep fried prawn

Yaki-soba – noodles fried with a variety of vegetable and meal fillings

Na no hana sarada – salad of rapeseed blossoms, a spring favorite

Goma-ae – side vegetables with sweet and savory sesame dressing, often spinach

Tebasaki – chicken wings

Izakayas are everywhere – just look for the red lantern! There are several big chains that helpfully provide illustrated, bi-lingual menus and are concentrated around major stations. Some of them are quite upmarket, such as Takewaka. http://www.takewaka.co.jp/en/index.html.

Head over to the JR train tracks around Yurakucho station to find scores of quality izakayas serving regional cuisine, including Hokkaido and Kyushu. For an unforgettable experience, try to get a table at Shin-Hinomoto (Andy's Fish).

2-4-4 Yurakucho, Chiyoda-ku, +81 3 3214 8021, andys-fish.com/Shin-Hinomoto. Open Mon-Sat 5pm-midnight, English spoken.

Andy's specialty is fish and he sources the best stuff daily from the Tsukiji market.

Get off at Yurakacho, take the BIC Camera exit, Hibiya. Turn left and follow the JR tracks across from the Yurakacho Denki building (or the Rose and Crown pub). Again, keep an eye out for the Guinness sign and Andy's lantern.

Shabu-shabu

A shabu-shabu restaurant is a Japanese temple of food and fun. How could one nation come up with so many ways to experience culinary joy? Still, here it is, another "must do" on your already dizzying itinerary.

The basic idea is to have a pot of clear stock with simmering mushrooms, leeks, tofu, and cabbage and a plate of very thinly sliced quality beef, often wagyu. Diners pick a slice of beef with chopsticks, submerge it for a few seconds in the simmering broth, then dip it in the sauce and let it melt on their tongue. Two types of sauce are served; ponzu (a mix of soy, citrus, dashi stock, and grated radish) and goma-dare, a sesame, soy, miso, and dashi-based concoction. One is refreshing and zingy, the other is savory-sweet, rich, and textured.

Diners will often go through more than one platter of beef. In fact, in answer to the diners' insatiable appetite, many shabu-shabu places offer "tabe-hodai", or "eat as much meat as you can within an hour or two".

Pork is another option for shabu-shabu, although less common.

Shabu-shabu places are everywhere, but to be sure, explore the gourmet floors of department stores. Along with sushi-ya, shabu-shabu restaurants are a common tenant of the restaurant floor.

Genkaya Shabu-Shabu Kan in Harajuku offeres shabu-sha-bu tabehodai.
>6-7-8 Jingumae, Harajuku
>Tel. 03-3406-6500

Yakiniku

Yakiniku restaurants offer do-it-yourself grilled meals of meat and vegetables. It might sound tiring, but the real joy of yakini-ku is wagyu, meat of prized Japanese cattle. People lay heavily marbled, tender slices of expensive meat to sizzle and smoke over individual grills sunk in tabletops. Within a minute or two, the meat is ready to be dipped into sauce and eaten. Wagyu is made for open flame, as smokiness brings out the sweetness in the fat. An easy way to go about ordering is to ask for "niku moriawase", a choice selection of meat.

Chicken and pork are also on offer and much cheaper than wagyu. As with shabu-shabu, many yakiniku restaurants offer a tabehodai option.

Beyond restaurants

The best-kept secret about Japan is that you don't need to go to a restaurant to eat well. The Japanese love eating, and love eating quality food. They are busy people. The combination makes for a country with countless food options that can be accessed on every step of your trip.

Trains and train stations

Japan is blessed with a world-class and vast train infrastructure. With the exception of Shikoku and the Okinawa islands, even the tiniest of hamlets can usually be reached by train. The Jap-anese travel a lot by train, and the hours spent aboard require nourishment. To meet the demand for food to be enjoyed along with the passing scenery, the art of making bento – boxed meals – has spawned a whole train-related branch, eki-ben (short for eki bento, bento meals sold at train stations, or "eki").

Each station will have eki-ben reflecting the cuisine of their region. Eating a "regional" eki-ben is an important part of the traveling experience, and department stores often hold "eki-ben fairs", promoting the food of different regions. Eki-ben are also sold onboard shinkansen trains. It pays to be prepared, though, and get the eki-ben before boarding the train, as the shinkansen trolley often sells out of them.

Typical eki-ben have plentiful rice, a variety of simmered, pickled,, and fried vegetables, and a number of meat, fish, or chicken morsels. Some are a bit more luxurious and feature fish roe. Prices hover somewhere between $6 and $14.

Convenience store

A Japanese convenience store is truly convenient. Convenience stores sell a lot of food, including fresh meals. There are bento boxes, salads, rows of onigiri rice balls, sushi, and sandwiches. At the counter, there is a crate of steaming oden from which the staff will pull out the simmered vegetables and meats of your choice. Chinese steamed buns ("nikuman"), and all sorts of

deep-fried foods - chicken, croquets, hash browns – are kept in warming cabinets. Warm canned tea and coffee are there as well.

If the meal you fancy needs a microwave, the staff will heat it up for you. In fact, it is possible to eat cheaply and relatively well on your travels by only patronizing convenience stores – but who would want to do that?

Conveniently, a selection of alcoholic beverages, anything from tetra packs of cheap sake to mini bottles of French Champagne, is awaiting the busy tourist.

Depachika

In Japan, a department store is not just a destination for fashion and home wares. Department stores, importantly, are an easy beacon for those searching for dinner or lunch in a strange city. Go to the upper floor and you will find a level, or several levels, of a well-curated choice of restaurants. There could be a fine-dining option or two, a sushi-ya, a shabu-shabu restaurant, an Italian restaurant, and more. Most will offer special set menus at lunch at affordable prices.

Go down the escalators and you will reach the basement food hall, the "depachika." The word is made up of "depato" (department store) and "chika" (underground). For any serious gourmand, depachika is the stuff food dreams are made of.

The floors heave with endless options for sampling local produce, sake, tea, and cooking. Gyoza stalls, tempura stalls, sushi stalls, shumai stalls, salad stalls, yakitori stalls, pickles stalls...and that's just the savory selection. Countless patisseries sell their best cakes and croissants. Sellers of traditional Japanese sweets, wagashi, and French chocolatiers display their wares side-by-side. Many offer free samples. There is a bakery and a fresh food market. Depachika are a fascinating window into the breadth of Japanese cuisine, and a budget option for an eclectic dinner back at your hotel. You can pick up a box of sushi, a bento, or a container of deli food sold by weight. A section selling sake and fine wine is reliably there, too.

Come near closing time (after 7 pm) and a lot of fresh food will be offered at discounted prices.

The depachika at Takashimaya, Daimaru, Mitsukoshi, and in Ginza, Matsuya department stores are particularly heavenly.

Daimaru Tokyo Station

Has a wide selection of sweets, with 50 brands represented.
Phone: 03-3212-8011
1-9-1 Marunouchi Chiyoda-ku Tokyo
Business hours: 10:00 a.m. – 8:00 p.m.
Open year around.
http://www.daimaru.co.jp/tokyo/
http://www.daimaru.co.jp/english/tokyo.html (English)

Matsuya Ginza

Famous for its wide selection of bento.
Phone: 03-3567-1211
3-6-1 Ginza Chuo-ku Tokyo
Business hours: 10:00 a.m. – 8:00 p.m.
Open year around
http://www.matsuya.com/foreign/index.html (English)
Mitsukoshi Nihonbashi

Phone: 03-3241-3311
1-4-1 Nihonbashi Muro-machi Chuo-ku Tokyo
Business hours: 10:00 a.m. – 7:00 p.m.
Open year around
http://www.mitsukoshi.co.jp/store/fcs/

Takashimaya Nanba

Phone: 06-6631-1101
1-5, Namba 5-chome, Chuo-ku Osaka
Business hours: 10:00 a.m. – 8:00 p.m.
Open year around
http://www.takashimaya.co.jp/osaka/store_information/index.html

Takashimaya Kyoto

Phone: 07-5221-8811
52, Shinmachi Nishiiru, Kawaramachi Shijodori, Shimo-gyo-ku, Kyoto
Business hours: 10:00 a.m. – 8:00 p.m.
Open year around
http://www.takashimaya.co.jp/kyoto/store_information/index.html

Michelin Guide in Japan

One of the oldest food guides in the world, Michelin Guide waited for more than 100 years before venturing into Japan. The first 2008 Japanese edition of the guide covered only Tokyo, awarding 191 stars, which was still more than Paris and New York held combined. Eventually, the Michelin Guide expanded to cover Yokohama, Shonan, Osaka, Kyoto, and Kobe (the latter three are part of the Kansai edition). Now, Japanese restaurants collectively hold 595 stars. 30 restaurants have been awarded 3 Michelin stars, in contrast with France's 27.

Unfortunately, the guide has been published only in Japanese for the past several years, but 2012 editions can still be purchased on Amazon. Otherwise, Michelin Guide now publishes a free online version via Gurunavi website: http://gm.gnavi.co.jp/home/.

Some of the 3 Michelin star restaurants from Tokyo Yokohama Shonan 2014 Guide:

Sushi Araki

5-14-14 Ginza, Chuo, Tokyo
Telephone 03 3545 0199
Open Mon, Tue, Thur-Sun lunch 12noon-2pm, dinner 6-8.30pm / closed Wed
Admission Set course ¥21,000- ¥26,250

Japanese Azabu Yukimura

Takayanagi bldg 3F, 1-5-5 Azabu-juban, Minato, Tokyo, Japan
Transport Azabu-juban station (Toei Oedo, Tokyo Metro Namboku Lines), exit 5a
Telephone 03 5772 1610
Open 5.30-8pm (LO)
Admission dinner ¥30,000-

Japanese Ishikawa

5-37 Kagurazaka, Shinjuku, Tokyo
Telephone 03 5225 0173

Open Mon-Sat 5.30pm-12midnight (L.O. 10pm) / closed Sun and nat. holidays
Admission ¥15,750

Modern French -Joël Robuchon

Ebisu Garden Place, 1-31-1 Mita, Meguro, Tokyo
Telephone 03 5424 1347
Open lunch 11.30am-2pm, dinner 6-9.30pm
Admission lunch ¥6,000, dinner ¥22,500
URL www.robuchon.jp/

Japanese - Koju

8-5-25 Ginza, Chuo, Tokyo
Telephone 03 6215 9544
Open Mon-Fri 5.30pm-1am (L.O. 11.30pm), Sat 5.30pm-12midnight/closed Sun, nat. holidays, middle of August, New Year holidays
Admission ¥13,650-¥15,750
URL www.kojyu.jp/

Modern French - Quintessence

5-4-7 Shirokane, Minato, Tokyo
Telephone 03 5791 3715
Open lunch 12noon-3pm, dinner 6.30-11pm / closed Sun
Admission lunch ¥7,875, dinner ¥16,800
URL www.quintessence.jp/

Sushi - Sukiyabashi Jiro Honten

Tsukamoto Building B1F, 4-2-15 Ginza, Chuo, Tokyo
Telephone 03 3535 3600
Open lunch 11.30am-2pm, dinner 5-9pm / closed Wed
Admission lunch ¥17,850, dinner ¥25,200

Holidays and Festivals

Matsuri

The word matsuri means "festival" in Japanese. But a Japanese matsuri is not just an ordinary festival. Of the two most common religions in Japan, Shinto is the oldest and is essentially the "native religion" of Japan. Shinto is a polytheistic religion loosely based on ancestor worship. Many families keep an altar at home with some of the remains of an ancestor and pray to him regularly for assistance in daily life. Every Shinto shrine is associated with at least one kami (god) which, in many cases, is simply the spirit form of someone famous who lived in that area long ago (perhaps an ancestor of one of the first families to settle in the area). During the year, people stop periodically at their local Shinto shrine to pay their respects to the kami enshrined therein, or to request the assistance of the Kami in various life affairs (some large shrines specialize in specific affairs such as success in business or love). Once a year, the kami is transferred to a portable shrine called a mikoshi which is then carried around the local streets in order to properly bless the area.

The vast majority of the matsuri are intended for the local populace, although pretty much all of them are open to random spectators. Some popular matsuri have taken on a life of their own and people travel from all over just to watch. Many of the more popular matsuri have some kind of unique twist that make them popular -- but one should keep in mind that the popular festivals are only a small handful out of the thousands that take place each year across all of Japan. Most prefectures and many of the larger cities have at least one major festival for which they are well-known.

Unlike holiday parades in the States, festivals in Japan are very participatory. While a non-local tourist isn't likely to be seen riding atop one of the floats (those are usually local residents selected based on their status within the local mutsumikai, or resident's organization), visitors are mostly welcome to mingle with the participants and may even be offered a chance to help carry the mikoshi. One should be aware that, in most cases, the mikoshi are actually mini-shrines honoring the local gods and are generally treated with respect (though there are a few notable exceptions). That said, these gods are all heavily into partying, and a matsuri is generally accompanied by a fair amount of alcohol consumption and plenty of noise.

Japanese Festivals and Other Events

Shogatsu (January 1-3, various locations)

During the first few days of the New Year, pretty much everything shuts down across Japan. During this time, many residents make their first visit to their favorite shrine to pray for success in the coming year and to purchase protective talismans. At some famous shrines, like the Meiji Jingu Temple in Harajuku (Tokyo), people wait for hours to make their offering and prayers – but, at least at Meiji Jingu, it's worth doing once because the entire front of the shrine is turned into a huge offering pit with armed police officers standing among the money (holding shields, of course, since most people seem to aim directly at the officers when tossing their coins). It's the only chance the Japanese have to throw something at the police without being arrested.

Seijin Shiki (second Monday in January, various locations)

This is a national holiday celebrating the "coming-of-age" of young men and women who turned 20 during the past year. Many young people dress up in fancy traditional outfits and visit their favorite shrine to pray. If you enjoy beautiful young girls in kimono, this is a must-see event. The best place in Tokyo to see plenty of kimono-clad girls is Meiji Jingu (Harajuku).

Setsubun (February 3, various locations)

This is a festival practiced by many Japanese at home. Traditionally, one throws roasted beans either out the door or at a family member wearing a devil mask while shouting, "Devil goes out, good luck comes in"! Some Buddhist temples such as Narita-san Narita City, Chiba Prefecture) hold events where they allow visitors to toss some beans. Get there early before the lines get too long.

Sapporo Snow Festival - Yuki Matsuri (early February, Sapporo, Hokkaido)

Large snow and ice sculptures are built in Odori Park in central Sapporo. The sculptures are also lit up at night. Some two million people from all over the world visit Sapporo each year to see the beautiful frozen artwork.

Hadaka Matsuri (third Saturday in February, Saidai-ji Temple, Okayama Prefecture)

There are various "naked festivals" held throughout Japan but this one is the most well-known. Thousands of men wearing only loincloths are doused with water and then struggle to gain control of one of two "lucky sticks" tossed into the crowd to thrust the stick into a box of rice. Spectator seats are available for a price... or just hang out with the crowd and be careful not to get trampled.

Takayama Matsuri (April 14-15, October 9-10, Takayama, Gifu Prefecture)

Various tall and brightly decorated festival floats are pulled through the older section of Takayama city. Many of the floats include animated mechanisms which are fascinating to watch. During the off-season, many of the floats can be seen at the Matsuri no Mori festival museum.

Hanami (late March to early May, depending on the location)

Hanami refers to the Japanese tradition of cherry blossom viewing. It is not a festival per se, but many companies and neighborhood groups stake out a space in their local park right around the time the trees are at maximum bloom and throw a day-long party. Ueno park in Tokyo is usually filled to capacity with drunken visitors due to the size of the park and the large number of cherry trees contained therein. The exact date when the trees bloom varies each year, depending on the location and the weather. Most Japanese weather reports include news on the "hanami front" as it moves up the country.

The blossoms only last a week so it's hard to predict when to be here, but if you hit the right date, it's well worth the effort.

Kanamara Matsuri (first Sunday in April, Kawasaki Daishi, Kanagawa Prefecture)

You won't find this festival in many guidebooks. The Wakamiya Hachimangu Kanayama Shrine has been known since the Edo period as a place to pray for fertility, marriage, and marital harmony. So it's only fitting that the local residents carry a mikoshi sporting a giant penis around the streets. You can also find numerous penis-based souvenirs to bring home, including whistles of various sizes cleverly carved out of wood.

Kanda Matsuri (weekend closest to May 15 in odd-numbered years, Kanda, Tokyo)

This is a traditional neighborhood festival gone viral. Many groups from surrounding areas carry their kikoshi through the streets in the Kanda area. This is probably one of the most well-attended festivals in all of Tokyo. There are generally other smaller events in the area over the week leading up to the big day.

Sanja Matsuri (third Saturday in May, Asakusa, Tokyo)

This festival honors the founders of Senso-ji, the entrance to which is probably the most photographed location in all of Tokyo. The festival takes place over three days when mikoshi from three different shrines are carried through the streets of Asakusa. Even though, technically, Japanese law enforcement has been cracking down on the public display of yakuza-style full-body tattoos... if that's what turns you on, this is definitely the festival you want to attend.

Gion Matsuri (July 17, Gion, Kyoto)

This is the grand-daddy of all Japanese festivals and is generally ranked as one of Japan's top three. Various celebrations are held on the days leading up to the big parade where 20-meter tall highly decorated floats are pulled through the streets of

Gion (which also happens to be famous for its many traditional geisha houses).

Bon Matsuri (late July to early September, various locations)

Bon refers to a time, usually in mid-August, where Japanese people travel to their hometowns to pay their respects to the graves of their ancestors. Most neighborhoods in Japan schedule a local festival around this time, some more elaborate than others. If you're traveling around Tokyo any time in July or August, you will likely run across any number of neighborhood matsuri blocking the streets and making a general ruckus. Most local festivals include one or more "street fair" days, where local merchants and restaurants sell food and drink from booths on the street and offer various kinds of games for the kids. There is usually also a portable shrine carried through the streets of the neighborhood by the local residents. In some locations, like Nakano-shimbashi (Nakano ward, Tokyo), the street fair is preceded by an open karaoke contest the night before. Many also include something called "Bon Odori", a special circular dance done to the beat of a taiko drum and only seen during the Bon season.

Nebuta Matsuri (August 2-7, Aomori Station, Aomori Prefecture)

This festival features large colorful floats that are lit up like lanterns at night and carried through the city streets.

Kanto Matsuri (August 3-6, Akita City, Akita Prefecture)

A "kanto" is a bamboo pole about 8 meters high from which 46 paper lanterns are suspended. Youths dressed in festival costume hoist these poles onto their hips, shoulders, and foreheads (no hands) as they parade through the city streets.

Boshita Festival (September, Kumamoto Prefecture)

This festival is unique in that there are no portable shrines being carried around or floats being pulled. Instead, small groups from various neighborhoods, businesses, schools, and other organizations parade through the streets, each accompanied by one or more decorated horses. The festival lasts for five days with the parade as the climax on the fifth day. The name of the festival (and its origins) are shrouded in controversy which, these days, is simple enough to look up on the Internet. Kumamoto prefecture, incidentally, is well-known for their horse sashimi (raw horse meat); is a must-try if you visit the area.

Shichi-go-san (November 15, various locations)

This is the day on which five-year-old boys and three- or seven-year-old girls dress in fancy traditional outfits and visit their favorite shrine to pray. If you have a child of the appropriate age, you can rent the clothing at just about any department store. Even if you don't have kids, hanging out at one of the larger shrines is sure to provide plenty of photo opportunities.

Chichibu Yomatsuri (December 2-3, Chichibu, Saitama Prefecture)

This is another of Japan's big-three festivals. Six large portable shrines (most as tall as a two-story building), each representing one section of the city, are pulled around the streets by young men and women. The main parade, beginning at Chichibu Shrine and ending near City Hall, takes place on January 3 against an almost constant backdrop of fireworks from dusk until just before midnight. Night-time is the time to go because each yatai (portable shrine) is decorated with hundreds of candle-lit lanterns. A small team of taiko drummers inside each Yatai provides constant background music to keep the blood flowing in the cold mountain air.

Yomawari (mid-December, various locations around Tokyo)

This is not a "festival" per se, but rather an interesting tradition that is being kept alive by various neighborhood groups. Long ago, homes and other buildings were made of wood and heated by fire (wood and then later kerosene). Since the buildings in Tokyo were built so close together, one spark from a fire not properly extinguished could easily destroy a major portion of the city. In order to remind people to extinguish their fires, one or two volunteers would walk the streets banging together wooden blocks and shouting, "Be careful with your fire" in the hopes of waking anyone up who might have dozed off with their fires still burning. Of course, most homes these days are built of concrete or steel and are heated with electricity. But the tradition gives the long-time residents of the area a chance to get together during the cold winter months – usually over a few glasses of hot sake.

Packing for Japan

It is often said to "bring half the stuff and twice the money" when traveling, but you're going to Japan and Japan means comfort. I've traveled comfortably in Japan, even in the countryside, with a backpack and a roller-type suitcase. Personally, I bring the size that's acceptable for carry-on, but check my bag for departure.

I find carrying everything on my back (like the travel experts encourage us to do in Europe) to be a burden. Travel is no time for aching backs and injured shoulders. I like to plan for ease of movement, and count on flat surfaces and elevators for roller suitcases in Japan. You should be able to roll your way around Japan quite easily. But please note: don't consider this as license to bring the kitchen sink. Japan's souvenirs are sure to tempt and delight, so pack sparingly to leave room for the return trip. I always pack an empty duffel back that always seems to be completely stuffed upon return.

For 1 week or 3 weeks I use the same checklist.

Comfortable walking shoes (often with laces)

Comfortable loafers or dressier slip-ons (for taking on and off easily)

Two long sleeve shirts (or blouses for the ladies)

Clean socks with no holes! (Don't forget - you may be taking your shoes off!)

Clothes:

- ❏ 5 shirts: long- and short-sleeve
- ❏ 1 sweater or lightweight fleece
- ❏ 2 pairs pants + 1-2 skirts
- ❏ 1 pair of shorts
- ❏ 5 pairs of underwear and socks
- ❏ 1-2 pairs of shoes
- ❏ 1 rainproof jacket with hood
- ❏ Tie or scarf
- ❏ Sleepwear
- ❏ Swimsuit

Money—your mix of:

- ❏ Debit card (for ATM withdrawals)
- ❏ Credit card(s)
- ❏ Hard cash (in $20 bills)
- ❏ Suica (purchase at Narita upon arrival)

Documents plus photocopies:

- ❏ Passport
- ❏ Printout of airline eticket
- ❏ Driver's license
- ❏ Student ID, hostel card, etc.
- ❏ Railpass/train reservations/car-rental voucher
- ❏ Hotel reservation confirmations
- ❏ Insurance details
- ❏ Guidebooks and maps
- ❏ Address list for postcards
- ❏ Notepad and pen
- ❏ Journal
- ❏ Daypack

Electronics—your choice of:

- ❏ Camera (and related gear)
- ❏ Mobile phone
- ❏ Portable media player (smartphone, iPod, or other)
- ❏ laptop/netbook/tablet

- ❏ Ebook reader
- ❏ Ear buds or noise-reduction headphones
- ❏ Chargers for each of the above
- ❏ Plug adapters
- ❏ Earplugs/neck pillow

Toiletries kit:

- ❏ Toiletries (soap, shampoo, toothbrush, toothpaste, floss, deodorant, sunscreen)
- ❏ Medicines and vitamins
- ❏ First-aid kit
- ❏ Glasses/contacts/sunglasses (with prescriptions)
- ❏ Sealable plastic baggies
- ❏ Laundry soap
- ❏ Clothesline
- ❏ Small towel/washcloth

If you plan to carry on your luggage, note that all liquids must be in three ounce or smaller containers and fit within a single quart-size baggie. For details, see www.tsa.gov/travelers.

Japanese Survival Phrases

How much does it cost?	ikuradesuka	I-Ku-Ra-De-ssKa
Hello	konnichiwa	Konn-Nee-Chee-Wa
Good morning	ohayougozaimasu	O-Ha-Yo-Go-Za-ee-Ma-ss
Good Evening	konbanwa	Konn-Bann-Wa
Good Night	oyasuminasai	O-Ya-Su-Mee-Na-Ssa-ee
Thank you	arigatougozaimasu	A-Ri-Ga-To-Go-Za-ee-Ma-ss
Where is ~ ?	~ dokodesuka	Do-Ko-De-ssKa
Restrooms	otearai	O-Te-A-Ra-ee
Bank	ginkou	geenn-Ko
Subway	chikatetsu	Chi-Ka-Te-Tsu
Train	densha	Den-Shya
Bus	basu	Bus
Station	eki	E-Ki
Do you speak English?	eigogawakarima-suka	Ei-Go-Ga-Wa-Ka-Ri-Ma-ssKa
Sorry/Excuse me	sumimasen	Su-Mee-Ma-Ssen
Ticket please	kippu kudasai	Ki-Poo-Ku-Da-Ssai
One way ticket please	katamichikippuku-dasai	Ka-Ta-Mee-Chee-Ki-Poo-Ku-Da-Ssa-ee
Round trip ticket please	oufukukippukudasai	O-U-Fu-Ku-Ki-Poo-Ku-Da-Ssa-e
Cash	genkin	Gen-Keen
Airport	kuukou	Ku-U-Ko-U
One	ichi	
Two	ni	
Three	san	
Four	shi	
Five	go	
Six	roku	

Seven	nana
Eight	hachi
Nine	kyu
Ten	jyu
Hundred	hyaku
Thousand	sen
Ten Thousand	man

Japanese Dining Survival Phrases

Before eating	itadakimasu	Ee-Ta-Da-Ki-Ma-ss
When finished eating:	gochisousamadeshita-De-sh Ta	Go-Chi-So-Sama-
Any recommendations?	osusumewa nandesuka Nan-De-ssKa	O-Su-Su-Me-Wa-
You decide (I'll leave it to you)	omakase	O-Mah-Ka-Ze
Do you have an English menu	ingrishumenyu ga arimasuka?	Inn-Gleesh-Men-Yoo-Ga-A-Ri-Ma-ssKa
May I have the check please?	okaike onegaishimasu	O-Kai-Ke-O-Ne-Ga-ee-Shee-Ma-ss
Can I pay by credit card?	kaadode daijyoubu desu ka?	
I can't eat ~~ , ~~	taberaremasen,	Ta-Be-Ra-Re-Ma-Sen
Egg	tamago	Ta-Ma-Go
Meat	niku	Nee-Ku
Squid	ika	Ee-Ka
Horse	uma	U-Ma
Pig	buta	Boo-Ta
Raw fish	sashimi	Sa-Shee-Mee
Table for one	hitoridesu	Hi-To-Ri-De-ss

Table for two	futaridesu	Fu-Ta-Ri-De-ss
Table for three	sannindesu	San-Neen-De-ss
Table for four	yonnindesu	
Table for five	gonindesu	
water please	mizuwokudasai	Mi-Zu-Wo-Ku-Da-Ssa-ee
Tasty	oishii	O-ee-Shee

Shitsurei-shimasu (shit-sue-ray she-mas): Literally, "I'm about to be rude". Use this if you bump into someone, step on their toes, or nearly trip them with your rolling bag in a crowded station.

Ojama-shimasu (o-jama she-masu): Literally, "I'm causing you trouble". You would use this upon entering a private home or anywhere that's not generally a public place. You wouldn't use it upon entering a restaurant, for example, because coming to the restaurant is normally not considered to intrude on the proprietor's privacy.

Gochiso-sama deshita (go-she-so-sama de-she-ta): This is a complement for a fine feast. You would use this when getting up to leave after eating at a restaurant or right after the meal when visiting someone's home.

Otsukare-sama deshita (o-tsu-ka-re-sama de-she-ta): This is a phrase commonly used when a coworker is leaving the office. Literally, it means something like: "you're honorably exhausted". It also makes a good substitute for the overworked "kampai" when drinking with friends – especially after work (when everyone is usually exhausted).

Tsumaranai mono desu (tsu-ma-ra-na-i mono de-s): This is the usual phrase used when handing someone a gift. In the typical tradition of Japanese humility, this phrase means: "here's something not all that interesting".

Join me!

Once a year in January I lead a small group on a budget-friendly 7 or 10 day tour around Japan. We kick things off with a professional-level guided sake tasting and brewery tour in Tokyo and then travel to historic Kyoto and Hiroshima via the famous "bullet train," sharing with you my favorite special, out of the way spots. I also take care to assemble an interesting, diverse, and compatible group so that we all come away with some new lifelong friendships and enjoy intense camaraderie along the way.

My goal for this trip is to keep expenses down by eating and sleeping like a temporary local – showing you that you can "get more by spending less" on your travels in Japan. Between food and accommodation I try to spend under $100/day including food and accommodation.

Where possible, we stay at traditional Japanese ryokan and eat simply, but this is Japan – so it's going to be wonderful – and we're looking to heighten our experience by sharing it with fellow travelers. It can't be emphasized enough that seeing Japan with this group has been the genesis of many lifelong friendships, much camaraderie, and tremendous enjoyment of Japan. Please join us.

If you are interested, please drop me a line at
jim@stewartsjapan.com
and I'll send you the complete itinerary and instructions
for joining this year's trip.

Spots tend to fill up by October, but send me an email and we'll see if there have been any cancellations.

Thank you!

I hope you enjoy this book, and I hope you enjoy your trip to Japan. If you have any questions, or want more help planning your trip please send me an email: jim@stewartsjapan.com

As an owner of this book you are entitled to a free PDF version of the city and brewery maps. Please send me an email with "PDF maps please" and I'll send them along.

Kampai!
Yours truly,
Jim Stewart

CPSIA information can be obtained
at www.ICGtesting.com
Printed in the USA
FSHW020502211019
63220FS